THE
Spiritual
COWBOY

GREG REID

Ordering Information:

Prime Seven Media
518 Landmann St.
Tomah City, WI 54660

Printed in the United States of America

CONTENTS

Acknowledgements...v

Chapter 1: The Taxi Driver and the Goanna 1

Chapter 2: My First and Second Visions 32

Chapter 3: The Drowning Chinese Girl 65

Chapter 4: The Rainbow Serpent 89

Chapter 5: Gan Gan NT 116

Chapter 6: The Quinkans 132

Chapter 7: The Wise Old Woman 161

Chapter 8: The Road Home 181

Poems

Land Rights 14

A Ringer 22

A Man Who Loves Horses 24

David...58

ACKNOWLEDGEMENTS

Help has come in many forms from the sublime to the divine. It occurred most notably 1994, when I wrote a letter to a Ngarinyin Law man in Derby in WA. asking him to teach me how to be a healer. His name was David Mowaljarlai. I'd never met this man before. All I knew was that he was the author of a book called *Yorro Yorro*. He replied to my letter by phoning me at my workplace saying, "Greg, you've asked to be a healer, know that it is already".

The effect that Dr. Stylianos Atteshlis (Daskalos) had on my life was like someone walking into a dark room and turning on a light switch. From 1990 with the release of the book *The Magus of Strovolos*, he has guided me like a loving father. In a sense, I've had three fathers in this lifetime; Daskalos, my birth father, and Yangarrinny Wunungmurra who gave me his last name and adopted me into the Dhalwangu tribe of the Yolngu Nation in North East Arnhem land. His son Maylia started the adoption process and he gave me the name "Dharayara". I am eternally grateful to Maylia and Yangarrinny for giving me access to another world.

My gratitude and thanks to Daskalos' daughter, Panayiota, for carrying on the legacy that her father bequeathed to the world.

My thanks to Daniel Joseph from America who also helps to carry the flame.

Heartfelt thanks to my family: my wonderful dad (Wally), my loving mum (Elaine) now deceased and my three siblings (Del, Andrew and Stuart).

Special thanks to my great sons of whom I am so proud and honoured to be called their father: Clinton, Sean and Ryan.

Finally, I would like to acknowledge Rosemary Maltos who has been the backbone behind this book. When I could not see my way forward at times, she was my eyes. Other times, she gifted me with a thought and still other times, she was the ink that flowed through my empty pen.

Thank you to everyone that has touched my life in one way or another.

CHAPTER 1

THE TAXI DRIVER AND THE GOANNA

It was a dark overcast morning with rain coming down as drizzle, as I drove up Mourilyan Road, Innisfail less than 24 hours after splitting up with my wife, one week before her birthday, March 1996. From out of the drizzling rain, a taxi driver appeared on the side of the road with his bag of onions. He didn't look for oncoming traffic. He just crossed the road directly into the path of the little maroon *Mitsubishi Lancer* that I was driving.

I only had time to put my foot on the brake for a few seconds and in a flash, he smashed against the bottom left-hand side of the windscreen. His head left about a 5-inch indentation on the screen and, being a laminated screen, it didn't break. I vividly recall seeing onions flying everywhere.

I stopped the car and rushed out to see if he was okay. I spoke to him and asked if he was alright but he didn't reply, so I shook him a little trying to get a response. However, he lay lifeless on the road. I started to panic thinking that he was dead. His skin felt cold. I then took his wrist to feel for a pulse but there was none. I placed my fingers under his chin on the carotid artery and there was no pulse there either. I tried once more on his wrist but there was nothing.

I sat with the taxi driver in the drizzling rain for about 10 minutes and out from the centre of my being I called out, "In the name of Jesus Christ I ask that this man be allowed to live." About 15 minutes after the accident, the ambulance arrived. I learned in the following days that his life had been spared. I was taken to the police station and tested for driving under the influence, but I was clean. I had no alcohol in my system. The police questioned me further about the incident and I was released with no charges.

The taxi driver recovered but there was talk that he was going to sue me. However, that never happened because I guess his legal people couldn't find anything on which to build a case. If he only knew that Christ gave him one more chance. Maybe he did know and that's why he never sued.

This is the first time that I have spoken the truth about this accident. Why have I waited 20 years to tell it? It is because, up until now, I was afraid that no one would believe me. Up until now, I dared not tell family members or friends simply because I ran the risk of being laughed at and derided. Well, I'm not afraid anymore.

It wasn't me who breathed life into the taxi driver. It was Christ. Others have raised people from the dead. For instance, St Spyridon of the Greek Orthodox Church is an example. A woman once came to him with a dead child in her arms, imploring the intercession of the saint. He prayed and the infant was restored to life. The mother, overcome with joy, collapsed lifeless but through the prayers of St Spyridon, she had her life restored.

Another time, hastening to save his friend who had been falsely accused and sentenced to death, the saint was blocked on his way by the unexpected flooding of a stream. He commanded the water, "Stop! For the Lord and all the world commands that you permit me to cross so that a man may be saved." The will of the saint was honoured and he happily crossed over. The judge believed a miracle had occurred. He received the saint with esteem and set his friend free.

What stopped me from believing that I had just witnessed a miracle all those years ago on Mourilyan Road when Mr Kassiotes had his life restored? I just hid it away and hoped I'd never have to deal with it. I believed that I was a sinner and wasn't worthy in God's eyes. I had simply committed too many sins to be taken seriously. Today, I believe that this kind of thinking holds us back from realising our true potential. I hope that by sharing my story it will help someone on his or her journey.

I am a very everyday Aussie, just a regular bloke, who grew up wanting to ride horses and become a ringer. I still see myself as much a part of Australia as the Brigalow trees I once rode through. Just add a touch of lemon-scented gum and mix in some horse sweat and you've got me in a nutshell. I drank plenty of beer along the way up until 2010, when I learned about moderation. I probably also had more than my fair share of relationships with the fairer sex. Yeah, I lived the Australian way of life to the max. The only difference is Christ interceded in my life and, at times, I didn't even know He was at work.

Let me start at what could be called the first miracle. The background is Central Queensland when I was about seven years old. My brother, Andrew, is with our dad on a cattle property and he is fixing a pump for pumping water for cattle. I can remember it as if it was yesterday. In fact, it was about 53 years ago. Dad is trying to fix this pump. It actually was a Villier's petrol motor, faded red in colour. Sometimes Dad could fix them; sometimes it took hours with bursts of swearing to pierce the silence. Dad had trouble fixing this one and Andrew and I were looking for an escape from our boredom.

With three of our working cattle dogs following and looking for mischief, we found some in the shape of a goanna (lizard). The dogs were in on the action pretty quick and quite soon, armed with sticks, Andrew and I soon put the goanna to eternal sleep. For some strange reason, I wanted to take the goanna home as some kind of trophy to show Mum or, maybe if the truth be known, give her a fright. I quite often took home bush flowers for her and she always expected something nice, but this day I thought I'd play a trick on her with a dead goanna.

The goanna had spent the whole day in the back of the truck and when we got home, I wrapped it up in my shirt and proceeded up the stairs of the house. My auntie was there, very pregnant at the time, and Mum was near the stove. I held out the goanna in my shirt and said, "Here, Mum, I have a surprise for you." At that point, the goanna jumped off onto the floor and came back to life trying to gain traction on the linoleum floor. People were screeching and screaming and my auntie nearly gave birth to the child there and then.

Somehow, it escaped everyone's attention that a goanna that had been quite lifeless all day long suddenly came back to life and the skeptics could immediately say that he was just concussed. However, I can tell you for certain he had parts of his brain hanging out. The fact that a dead goanna had just come back to life seemed quite normal to me.

These things would follow me all my life and still I would deny them. Why? I felt that I wasn't worthy. After all, I was a sinner and I had done things in my life which I was not proud of. I, therefore, figured that God would eventually find someone else, who was more worthy. The "eventually" never came but he kept knocking on my door saying, "When you're ready to have me in your life, I'll take you places you've never seen."

"I stand at the door and knock, and if you will open, I will enter and abide with you – I and the Father." (Revelation 3:20)

My biggest mountain to climb was to figure out if I was a healer or a sinner. It took nearly a lifetime to figure out that I was both. Some people may fall for the same trap that I did: trying to be perfect like Him. But it isn't a trap because we are meant to become like Christ. I think the best way to stay out of that *trap* is to acknowledge our frailties/weaknesses/sins etc. and along the way let Christ transform us to that perfection.

The Researchers of Truth state that everything in existence is energy vibrating at a certain frequency, including rocks, walls, water, and everything in existence. Quantum physics is now proving what mystics have known for millennia. They are acknowledging that there are parallel worlds of existence. There are other worlds vibrating, just at a different frequency from ours.

Learn how to vibrate at that frequency and you can visit other levels of existence. This can include other worlds such as the astral planes each consisting of seven planes (levels) and seven subplanes and each with its own unique frequency. I o

The lower astral world is where we go when we dream and when we die. The indigenous people of Australia call this world Dreamtime. They refer to Dreamtime as a state that has always been and always will be. The higher realm of the astral world is the five-dimensional world. It is the most rarefied of the three worlds of separation. Some people call it the world of thought (mental level).

If you get your body to vibrate at a certain frequency, you can pass through a material wall. This is because the wall is not solid. It is mostly empty space. Most things we see as solid are 99% empty space. We all have a specific frequency. Just like a radio station, we all transmit on a specific frequency. You could say that we are all miniature radio stations. Sufis call this frequency our *tome* and that's why sometimes when we meet a fellow human being on a similar journey, we connect straight away. Like attracts like – oil comes to oil, water to water.

Many say the worlds beyond the three dimensional planes of Earth are far more real than the reality that we can experience with our five senses. Ask the Aboriginal people of Australia about the little (spirit) hairy men or the Wandjina spirit beings.

In essence, our whole life is made up of what we think. Buddha said, "What we are today comes from our thoughts of yesterday, and our present thoughts build our life of tomorrow. Our life is the creation of our mind."

There are over 25 visions that have filled my life so far. Some of them have just appeared out of nowhere with no explanation and with no instructions. You'll find some of them scattered throughout this book and I will share some of what I've seen beyond the veil.

I was born in July 1955, in a little town in New South Wales called Kyogle. I can't tell you much about the place since I've only been through the town once since I was born. However, I do know my parents named me after one of the sisters there: Sister Gregory.

My parents were dairy farmers and every morning around 4 AM, they carted me off to the dairy while they milked the cows. They milked by hand in those days and around 40 cows were milked most mornings. Being only a few months old, I took a dislike to being left on my own and hollered my lungs out to gain attention. My parents told me the only time I'd settle down was when the radio was on. Maybe that's played a part in my career as a radio announcer. It is something that I've been doing for over 20 years. It was certainly not my first choice of vocation but that is a whole other story.

We got out of the dairy business when I was about two. There was no happier kid in town than me. The family sold the dairy business and bought two cattle properties in Central Queensland. It was in a little town called Comet that I did the bulk of my growing up. Some could say that I'm still growing up today. I would take that as a compliment.

Comet was a town of about 20 houses. It was once a thriving centre with numerous pubs since it was the railhead that took the wool from Western Queensland to the coast. This was back in the day of the bullock wagons and I am told even camels. However, that was before my time. All that was left was a pub, general store and a school. It included four Reid kids, a big mob of Doyle kids, the Williams brothers, Ruth Saunders, and the school teacher. I completed year one to year seven at Comet State School.

There was something different about me right from beginning. At age two, my mum came down the steps of our high blocked home and found me playing with a red-bellied black snake. I had it in my hands and for some reason it didn't bite me. The red-bellied black snake is the 10th deadliest snake in Australia and I had him for a plaything.

The dead goanna was still some years away. We lived in a typical country town with Aboriginal friends as playmates and, at that time, we didn't know they were different from us. They were just our mates. My one great love growing up was riding horses. My dad let me indulge in this practice and at age four, I was let go on my own. The only problem was that the horse took off and at this young age, I didn't know much about control.

I came off the runaway horse and fell into a pile of sticks under a big black wattle tree. Unknown to me, some of the sticks found their way into the back of my neck where they conveniently stayed for nearly 20 years until a doctor found them during an examination.

I was crying my lungs out and Dad, being the great diplomat that he was, was trying to get me to shut up. He kept saying, "Stop crying or Mum will get mad." Suffice it to say, Dad was more worried about his dilemma with a cranky wife than the sticks in the back of my neck. No doctor, just a wash down with some Dettol and Dad missed his ear bashing which I feel in retrospect was totally due.

That was lesson number one. Number two was just around the corner. This time I had graduated to about age seven and was getting the milking cow and calf into the yard to separate the calf from its mother. The cow needed to be milked so that we would have fresh farm milk the next morning. I was soon to be nominated as the chief farm boy to do the milking. At that point, we even separated the cream from the milk and made butter with it. The separator removed the cream from the milk. It required a steady hand to produce two curls in the cream in the output spout of the separator. Less than two curls and the cream was too thick. More than two curls and the cream was too thin. That's the exact consistency we needed to make the butter. When I milked the cow, I generally managed two thirds of a bucket which was very heavy for an eight-year-old to carry. It wasn't too long before I was in the building trade making a go-cart to carry the milk. It was crude but it showed early signs of my resourcefulness to adapt and make the most of a situation.

One day, I was getting the milking cows in. I let them go a good way ahead so I could kick my horse with my heels and catch them up to them, flat out at a canter just as they were reaching the yards. Of course, the canter was the adrenaline rush and the high point of the afternoon. It was my little secret. Everything was going according to plan, except for one day when the horse shied at something in the long grass and I was thrown off. I was riding bareback which means that my little butt was glued to the horse's hide with no saddle.

The horse's name was Echo. To this day, I don't know what spooked him but I was totally concussed. I was only discovered late in the afternoon by the mere fact I hadn't come home at the usual time. I was put to bed and, from my recollection of it, didn't wake up until the following afternoon. Twenty-four hours concussed and not one visit to the doctor.

I've since come to understand that riding horses is much like negotiating life and everything it entails. Once a horse has bucked me off in a certain way, I learn that lesson. I believe it's like that in life, too. We have the opportunity to learn from our mistakes in a similar way.

Needless to say, I found new and spectacular ways to fall off. However, I also became what was considered to be a really good rider with no fear. I have written numerous poems about some of these escapades and I have shared some of them with you in this book.

Next to my love of horses, came my great love of country music, especially the songs of Slim Dusty. He had just recorded the song that would become Australia's first top-10 song ever overseas.

This happened in England. I was about eight years old at the time and had just bought a red HMV battery record player. My first record was his song *A Pub with No Beer,* which had on the same EP (extended play), three other songs.

This was when the old 78s, which were breakable, were being replaced by the vinyl 45 singles and 33⅓ speed albums. I played this record over and over so many times that, in fact, I believe it influenced my family in a way that they all have a distinct dislike for Slim and still do to this day.

But I heard the heart of the country in Slim's music. He sang about the stock horses and the brumbies. He put one of our most famous poems to the music of *The Man from Snowy River.* He was able to take me on that famous ride and make me feel like I was really there. He sang the poems of Lawson, Patterso, and of the great ballad writer Stan Coster.

He sang about the drovers, ringers, yard builders, truck drivers and indigenous stockmen. He also sang about the wild-eyed scrubber cattle stampeding in the middle of the night and of the brave men who went to steady the lead of this wild mob. He sang of Trumby, the indigenous stockman, who died after drinking poisoned water that was intended to kill dingoes. There was a sign on the tree warning everyone that the waterhole had been poisoned. However, poor Trumby couldn't read or write and drank the water.

My heart went out to this fictitious Trumby and to all the indigenous people who couldn't read and write at that time. The song resonated in a part of me that I that I still hold very dear. I have no doubt that it influenced my decisions in later life that have seen me work in Aboriginal organisations for 18 years. Thank you, Trumby.

At the end of the day, many things have shaped my destiny. As long as I can remember, I've had an awareness that Christ is within me. It is only at this point in my life that I feel free to be able to share some of the incredible experiences that I've witnessed. Edgar Cayce looked at it this way, "In all nature the Spirit of creation is emanating, and one who attunes self in mind or mental forces towards beings of emanation, gains knowledge in an inestimable manner, that become the soul, the personality, the being of the individual." (Cayce Reading 345-2)

I will take many falls off my "horse of life" in search of that goal, but with each one, I will learn another valuable lesson. It would be probably fair to say that most of my learning has happened in the last 10 years. It is more than all the learning I experienced in the previous 50 years. Was I a slow learner? I don't think so. It's all about timing. When you're ready, you're so thirsty you're like a desert that hasn't seen rain in the last thousand years. When the floodgates open, you're ready to savour every last drop.

At age nine, I was allowed to go with the big men mustering on a big property called Nine Mile. It included 14,700 acres that was all in one block apart from the bullock and horse paddocks. One nine-year-old boy, on his own at times, in a 14,700 acre paddock on an ex-brumby horse – this was the real deal. We were mustering and there were wild cattle called scrubbers among them. Most of these cattle had rarely seen a human being and apart from being wild, if cornered, they had the ability to kill you. If they didn't kill you, they could do some real serious damage. They mainly wanted to run and to flee from the danger. However, if they were cornered. they could turn on you like a snake.

I was on my first trip out mustering cattle when someone yelled out, "Piker bullock!". In 0 to 5 seconds, my old ex-brumby horse was in top gear. I had no way to hold him. All I could do was hang on for dear life. I was a nine-year-old child riding out on the wing of the herd on a horse that had just hit overdrive. We finally got the bullock into the mob of cattle we called "coachers" and guided them back to the holding paddock which completed a successful day. The main stockyards were built to hold these wild cattle. They were seven feet high, which was a foot higher than any normal stockyard around at that time. These stockyards never had one beast escape.

I know that we were in the business of chasing and catching wild cattle, but one afternoon they captured the oldest, meanest and wildest bull they were ever able to get their hands on. They weren't actually too keen to get their hands on him at all. In fact, no one was even game to get into the yard with him.

When it got dark, I went down to the yards and sat there for ages. I felt at one with this bull. I felt his urgency to leap over the top rail of those yards and to savour the taste of freedom again. I kind of felt guilty thinking this way but my mind and the bull were as one. He didn't run at the fence and try to charge me. Somehow, the bull seemed to know what I was thinking.

Of course, I didn't tell a soul what I was thinking. I just had my dinner and went to bed. The first thing the next morning, I was down at the yards and you guessed it, the bull was gone. He didn't even break a rail going over the top. In fact, he didn't leave any hair behind where his back legs may have scraped over the rail.

He had managed to clear seven-foot fence without even touching the top rail. The men were aghast. They couldn't believe his feat. It was like some ghost came in the middle of the night and helped him over. My dad has not spoken to me about that bull again.

Nine Mile was a special place for me. I had this feeling straight away as a seven-year-old boy that I had walked many parts of this land before. I have looked back on my past when I have accessed the Akashic Records (also called the Cosmic Consciousness) and found that some of my incarnations on planet Earth have been as an Aboriginal man and, sometimes, as an Aboriginal woman. In a way I had come back home. It was the country I had once walked and held a deep connection with.

I walked with my two brothers down an ancient trail of what was once a Bora ceremonial ground. One picture has me bending over putting stones back to where they once belonged. I seem to know exactly where they should be. I still have the black and white photo today. The Bora ceremonial ground also had a profound effect on my younger brother. I will walk that walk again the day I pass to the other side. There is a special ceremonial ground waiting for me, complete with Bendee trees acting as guardians.

It was on this property that I also had my first out-of-body experience. I was nine at the time and I was riding out from the back dam with the smell of lemon-scented gum in the air. I was on my way to the ceremonial ground, even though I wasn't supposed to be going that way. I rode along, with not a care in the world. Up above, circled a big Wedge Tail Eagle. Somehow, I seemed to have left my body and became at one with the Eagle. Some call this practice examatosis. I have since learned how to do this consciously and have done so many times. I did come back into my body and proceeded on with my journey. I did not really understand what had just happened. It is important to note that there are safe ways and unsafe ways to do this. My guides have been my Maker, Daskalos of the Researchers of Truth, and numerous archangels.

As a child, I was absorbing most things around me. I had this deep connection with the land. I was a part of it and it spoke to me. I'll speak of that connection with a few lines from a poem I wrote about it. It's a special connection that I still feel to the land and intermingled with it is the struggle the Aboriginal people had to go through to gain their land rights. In Australia, we believe we own the land. From an Aboriginal perspective, they believe the land owns them and they have certain obligations to take care of it.

Land Rights

It's just finally dawned on me
Why the Aboriginals lay claim to
    land;
It's not land as we see it that
    they want
This they don't demand.

It's not land with dirt and grass
These humble people seek;
It's the spirit part, like a temple
They cry for their soul to keep.

It's a bit like saying here's a
    church
But you can't go in to pray;
We've dispossessed their spirit
    from the land
A land they did obey.

The meek and humble shall
    inherit the earth
They taught me at Sunday
    School;

This land they will inherit one
    day
Or you can call me a fool.

I feel this special empathy
For this land they call home;
Lived here for 100,000 years
Then no more we'd let them
    roam.

I feel this special harmony
When I climb up on my mare;
The red hide reins are my hymn
    book
The congregation, trees and
    fresh air.

That's why the land is sacred
To them and also me;
If you can respect how we do
    our praying
We'll solve this land rights
    problem easily.

This was my sacred place, my place of praying, and my connection to my Maker. I struggled with the "regular church" and still do. The closest that I've come to attending one these days is listening to Joel Osteen on the TV.

I gave my life to Christ in 1989. I've always been a believer but I didn't give myself completely to Jesus as I did in 1989 at Kurramine Beach. That night I had a conscious out-of-body experience (OBE). I went back into the Akashic Records (Cosmic Consciousness) to the night when Judas betrayed Christ in the Garden of Gethsemane. The only way I can describe it is as if I am sitting and watching a movie. Then all of a sudden, I find myself I'm in the movie. Years later, I saw some trees at a friend's place in Deniliquin and asked what kind they were. Leonie my friend replied, "they're olive trees." I explained that I had seen them somewhere else. I didn't dare say that I had seen them in a state of examatosis, otherwise called an OBE. After that event, I looked on the Internet and got books out of the library just to double check that olive trees actually grew in that area. I found out that olive trees were common in that part of the world. That night I said, "Christ, I give my life to you."

My childhood was jam-packed, full of new adventures and there was always plenty to do. Being the oldest boy, I got the bulk of the jobs that us kids needed to do. My sister wasn't included in the work gang. In the 60's, 240v electricity wasn't yet available to us. We had a 32v system that ran the lights and the washing machine. We also had a copper boiler in which we boiled hard-to-wash clothes, using fire underneath to heat the copper bowl. We also had a wood stove and with my Mum's obsessiveness with cooking, the wood supply was always running critically low. You guessed it – I did the bulk of cutting the wood. My middle brother, Andrew, was always conveniently missing. These days it would be called laziness.

My youngest brother, Stu, wasn't quite up to swinging the axe. However, when it got to that point, he would also conveniently go missing, especially when the wood needed to be chopped. That was only half of it, since the cows needed to be milked every morning. They needed to be separated from their calf in the afternoons so the family could have milk in the morning. Otherwise, the calves drank all of the available milk overnight. In addition to a pretty busy work schedule for a young boy, there were the ever-endless requests to rake up the leaves and collect rotten mangoes that had fallen to the ground from the many trees that made up our rather large backyard.

My mum bordered on Obsessive Compulsive Disorder (OCD) or maybe she just completely climbed the ladder and crossed to the other side. Anyway, she was obsessive and I always seemed to be in the firing line when it came to tidying up. The other two happily started out with me and within about 10 minutes, they were somewhere else on the planet. This all seemed to escape my mother. As long as the job got done, nothing else mattered. What stopped me from throwing in the towel somehow eludes me to this day.

We lived in a house with a huge backyard consisting of five mango trees, a custard apple tree, a mulberry tree, and a couple of citrus trees. I raked that backyard many times and I can still visualise where each mango tree was situated. I got a little industrious – instead of throwing the mangos away, I used to sell them for 25 cents a dozen. Since our house fronted the Capricorn Highway, I did a good business.

There was also the duck business. I would order 50-day-old ducklings from Brisbane on the plane. It would require a special trip to Emerald to pick them up off the plane. I had built a big pond for them under a mango tree. It had taken me a number of months to achieve this feat. It held water in a very dry climate with Mother Earth grabbing every available drop of water being offered, at every opportunity.

The reason I bought 50 ducklings was the predators including: the goannas, snakes, and ever-present cattle dogs. They were the bane of my life being a duck farmer at age eight. Most years, six or seven survived out of the 50 and they were destined to die because I used to sell them to people in the town.

Intermingled with all the work, was the play. My favourite thing to play was Cowboys and Indians. That's when the Doyle kids would come over along with the Watson kids and the Williams brothers, and just about any spare kid in town. We had cap guns and rifles, but the problem was that most of the kids wanted to play the part of the cowboys and I quite often ended up being the lone Indian.

This was a period when TV was just being introduced and The Lone Ranger was on. We didn't own a TV, so we had to go over to the neighbours to get our dose. I tried in vain to get my horse to do things like Silver, the Lone Ranger's horse. Silver could stand up on his back legs, but obviously my horse never watched the TV show. Therefore, she couldn't understand my instructions. From my perspective, Silver was the coolest horse on the planet.

Under the shade of the mango trees, we also played with toy animals (especially cows and horses) just like our dad who worked with cows and horses. We built fences out of sticks for them and yards to hold them in. In fact, everything was just about a dead replica of what the big people were doing. We were the stockmen, at least I was, and I just couldn't wait until I was back on a horse again. When these opportunities arose, they were like gold and I treasured every one of them. I would usually ride three miles to a place called St. Albans, which was a little property we had near the town. We had another one called Over the River and then the one of my dreams, Nine Mile. It was 14,700 acres of pure wild land, with not one acre touched by man.

I would often get to ride by myself on the property "Over the River". One day after we had had a big wet season, the billabongs were all starting to dry up. They had only about a quarter of their original amount of water. Much to my surprise, a good number of Yellow Belly fish were among them. They had little water and air left at the bottom of the billabong. I dismounted from my horse and caught some in my hat. Luckily, it had a hole in it since it was quite old. As a result, the water ran out and the fish stayed in.

I managed to catch nine that day. The only place I could think of to carry them home was inside my shirt. So, I rode about four miles home with a shirt laden with fishes. I was quite dismayed when I got home to be told they wouldn't be any good as they had been out of the water too long and wouldn't keep refrigerated. I hadn't figured that one out at the time. I just couldn't believe my good luck with all these fish in the bottom of a billabong. To this day, it's probably the most fish I've ever caught in one go.

The cattle that came from this property were so wild and so untouched by civilisation, that they would drop dead in the cattle yards at Comet when the train blew its loud whistle. This was back in the era of the steam train. These poor cattle were frightened out of their minds to hear such a sound that they dropped dead on the spot. The ones who boarded the train were destined for hamburger mince. The US wanted lean meat, Australia was just getting in on the act, and McDonalds was just starting to get a foothold in this country. But every player wanted lean meat and we still walk down that road today.

I think my dad said that he mustered about 300 head off the property and, being cleanskin cattle, we didn't have to pay for them in the first place. All we had to do was brand them and they were legally ours. The 300 free cattle helped get our family off to a good start in Central Queensland.

During this period, my mum used to get sick often and would need to go to Rockhampton to see the doctors. There were also numerous times when she would have to stay in the hospital. None of us kids really knew what was wrong except that we had to stay at our grandparents and that was okay. We had a roof over heads but we also had Granddad to contend with. He is probably the strictest man I've ever had to deal with to this day. There was no doubt, that with three extra children to care for, we only helped to increase his already over-the-limit blood pressure.

If we didn't do exactly how he wanted things done, Granddad would appear out of nowhere with a jockey whip with no leather at one end. This was the end with steel poking out and the end that came in contact with my legs as I danced a corroboree dance that few had ever seen before. This was no ordinary discipline. This was barbaric as he vented his frustrations on my two skinny little legs. The news was always at 6 PM and we had to be washed and presentable at the table by 6 PM. It was a case of "shut up and keep your elbows off the table." I don't ever recall him saying a kind word to me. That was left to Grandma. Maybe he did, but my mind won't let me remember.

I do remember, though, causing him some angst as I tried to conduct a rodeo with the milking cow's calf after we had herded them up in the yard. Some of the Doyle kids would be there, the Williams brothers, my middle brother, and the show was on. Once in the yard, we would get some hay rope, wrap around the calf, use another one as a kicking strap to make him buck, and then open the gate and spur him or her as the case would be. What once were quite placid milkers, the cows and calves were now somewhat aggressive rodeo stock. We used one of the kids as a lookout to keep an eye out for Granddad in order to quickly round up the calves and put them in their pen. Of course, there was a group of us sitting around looking totally innocent.

The Doyle kids were Aboriginal but we didn't know that. We didn't even seem to notice that they were black and we were white. They were just our friends and our school buddies. I think their mother, Colleen, had about 16 or 17 children altogether. The father was Gerry and my dad used to call him "Dig." Whatever that meant, I have no idea but I gather it was an affectionate term back in those days. There were also words used affectionately like Bungie, Buck, and others. At that time, "Yackeye" was the absolute ultimate word for having fun. I don't hear much of that word anymore which saddens me. The assimilation that the white nation had longed for, reached out her long tentacles and suffocated the "Yackeye."

The chief impediment in my life, apart from Grandpa, was the continued presence of snakes: Eastern Brown, Western Taipan, Red Bellied Black, King Brown snakes, Death Adders, and there were even a few tree snakes for good measure. Five of these snakes are in the 10 most deadly snakes list in Australia and don't for a moment believe that story that if you leave the snake alone, it'll go its own merry way. A Western Taipan that measured 6' 7" had a go at me. He was a monster and very aggressive. I've even had some rear up and tried to strike my horse as I was cantering along. To make it even worse, our house was an old Queenslander. There were no fly screens in those days and snakes could come in through the louvres at nighttime. For a young kid, some nights were difficult to get off to sleep fearing a snake would come through the louvre again.

We even had an Eastern Brown come through the louvres in the kitchen while we were all at the table having a meal. I can remember it just like yesterday. Strangely though, none of us were ever bitten by snakes, although we had a healthy respect for them, even today. I actually tasted snake in Arnhem Land and in China. It was kind of getting a bit of my own back.

A dramatic change was about to come about in my life. I was packed off to a boarding school: Rockhampton Boys Grammar. Coming from a life of perceived freedom, I thought I'd landed in jail. We weren't allowed out of the school grounds unless we had special leave. In addition, my family was about 275 kilometers away and rarely visited. I was 12 years of age and like that wild bull that escaped from the yards when I was about eight years old, I felt that I also wanted to escape this boarding school.

All I wanted in life was to become a ringer. Where I come from, a ringer was the real thing: he knew a horse, he knew how to ride flat out to the lead – he was the real deal. A stockman is a more sedate variety working on a big property, probably with intentions of becoming a manager. He wasn't a risk- taker like a ringer. He quite often was working his way up the corporate ladder. By contrast, the ringer was happy just loving what he was doing. For him, life was complete. He could muster wild cattle, do a droving trip, work in the yards dipping and branding, break a horse in, plait a green hide rope, kill a bullock and cut him up, pull a drought-starved cow out of a bog and even help a cow give birth. I became that ringer.

A Ringer

I've ridden flat out through the brigalow and yellow wood,
I've cursed the Lignum of the South West.
I've ridden boldly without fear,
I've ridden with the best.

I've ridden with both arms gashed open
I've felt no pain because adrenalin was my guide.
When sweat, blood and dust become one,
And you're married to horses hide.

I've tasted sweet quart pot tea,
From the clay pan water hole.
I've slept beneath the western skies,
And I've allowed them to steal my soul.

I've been one of rare breed, a slowly dying race;
If you look past the dust and the bush fly,
in the corner of my eye,
You'll find a ringer engraved in
every line on my face.

I was bright at school and I was dux of my class in year nine. However, that just added fuel to the fire of this idea that my mum had. She wanted me to become a lawyer. While I've got nothing against lawyers as such, I just wanted to become a ringer. Ringers didn't normally grow up and own property, and become *someone*. I felt that an unfair expectation rested on my shoulders. I was expected to be dux of my class again in year 10, so to prove everyone wrong I didn't try as hard. When the marks came out, I was number three in my class. When the lawyer business wasn't going to happen, my mum turned her focus on having me attend the Emerald Pastoral College.

The closest I ever got to becoming a lawyer was getting into trouble over an appointment with the headmaster. There were three of us, who were all in hot water. I figured that if I spoke on our behalf, I would be able to keep the story straight and true. Well, it wasn't actually straight and true. It was a lie but I was able to convince the headmaster many times before and I thought why not give it another go? As I tried to speak on behalf of the other two, he said, "Shut up, Greg, what do you think you are, a bush lawyer?" Considering the circumstances I was involved in, I didn't exchange this information with my mother. She must've seen something of a lawyer inside me that I didn't see.

The whole problem for me was that I had not been given a choice of the career I wanted. The choices were being made on my behalf. It seemed that I only had a small part to play in what was my life and my career decisions. I'm glad I didn't become a lawyer because I always felt there would come a time when I would be asked to defend someone who committed a murder. It's a situation like that I would have to make this ghastly decision on whether to chase the dollar or allow my conscience to be at peace.

I finished year 9 at Rockhampton Grammar School in 1969 and headed straight to Charters Towers to a property where we had cattle on assignment. We did this because our area was in the middle of the biggest drought since records began. Finally, I was doing some really meaningful stock work. One morning around 4 AM, I was awakened by the sound of horses squealing. In the pitch, black dark I went down towards the front gate to where our stock horses had gathered and outside I could just make out the outline of a Brumby stallion. I went up to the fence, held my hand out and he came up, smelled my hand, turned on his heel, and was away like the wind. I had this connection with horses that is very difficult to explain in words. I tried to do this in a poem called *A Man Who Loves Horses.* In later years, I interviewed on radio the original horse whisperer, Monty Roberts. I also sent him via email a copy of this poem. He replied from America that this particular poem encouraged him to make the world a better place for horses and for people.

A Man Who Loves Horses

Any man who loves horses
Must be a friend of mine;
For to love a horse properly
You start by being kind.

A kindness they can smell
When you reach out with your
*   hand;*
But it has to come from within
Or they'll know you're the wrong
*   man.*

I believe it is the highest love
any man can possess;
We can fool humans sometimes

The creator only chose a few
This special gift to bestow;
You can't pick it from the
*   outside*
Only a horse can know.

Only a man who loves a horse
Can transform the two into one;
Only he can savour the smell of
*   horse sweat*
When the time to ungirth has
*   come.*
But a horse never needs to
*   guess.*

I finished my year 10 at school, having achieved high marks in all but one of my grades: Science B. Strangely, quantum physics interests me now more than it ever did at school. I went home to work on the family property called "Fermanagh" which is about three hours inland from Rockhampton. I turned 16 in July of that year and I was nearing the height of my physical prowess. I was just as lean as lean could be. I could lift a 180-pound bag of wheat from the ground onto the back of a Toyota Land Cruiser by myself. I had imagined I was also at the height of my skills on the back of a horse or, more to the point, on the back of a wild horse.

We owned three stock horse mares that had just recently been broken by Johnny Chambers and two of them were given to me to educate. I was about to get the education. Mavis was her name and our paths were set to meet one afternoon that will remain forever etched in my mind. This was before the period of Monty Roberts and his famous "Join Up Method." This is what people have been doing in the outback for the past 200 years. To break a horse in was to break his spirit and then have him be subservient to you. Breaking them in was the first part, and then came the education: taking them out alongside older horses to help calm them down and gently working with the reins so that his or her mouth didn't become hardened by your touch. The ideal stock horse had what we called a "soft mouth."

The afternoon arrived. I put the bridle on her head, a saddlecloth on her back so she wouldn't be chafed by the saddle and finally a little poley saddle. I tightened the girth and walked around to make her feel more at ease so I could tighten the girth just that little bit more. I put my left foot in the stirrup iron and glided my right leg over her rump and into the offside stirrup iron. Mavis came from a long line of horses that knew how to buck. The "Lolly" breed of stock horse was known throughout Central Queensland for their brilliance at stock work but they came with a subtitle: They Really Can Buck. If you could get the best of one, you would have one of the best stock horses in the land.

It was only seconds before I came to a complete understanding that this one could buck. I must've lasted 60 seconds when she plastered me all over the stockyard rails. I got my breath, caught Mavis again, tightened the girth a little bit tighter, and eased into the saddle once more.

I lasted about 90 seconds this round before she ejected me and the saddle ingloriously into the dirt. I retreated momentarily, rolled a cigarette, and weighed up my options: Mavis 2, Greg 0. There was only one decision to be made. I made my way to Mavis and collected the reins. I tightened the girth for the third time and sucked in some deep breaths. I didn't want to let her know that deep down inside I was scared. I moved around her confidently, doing my best to let her know that I really wanted to become her friend. In moments like these, a boy can become a man and this was that moment. The decision that I made next would define much of how I later faced my adult life and that was the doggedness of never giving in.

My RM Williams boot slid into the nearside stirrup and all in one motion, my right leg glided over her rump once again and, just like radar, my right foot found the stirrup iron just as Mavis was leaving the ground. She bucked so high I thought we were going to reach heaven. I thought that she might even buck herself clear out of her own hide. She sucked back and tried every trick there was in the horse-bucking book but I stuck to her like glue. I followed every move she made and, eventually, I rode her to a standstill.

Unbeknown to me, Terry Rae from Dalgety's, a stock agent from Emerald, had been outside the stockyards in his car and he had just witnessed the whole event. Let's put it this way. He'll never forget the day I rode Mavis. With a few little hiccups along the way including a broken collarbone, Mavis and I became as one. To this day, I've never ridden a horse that was even half as good.

At home, I was earning $20 a week and a promise somewhere along the line that Dad would help me buy a property of my own. For the moment, it was $20 a week, plenty of sweat, and we worked six days a week. By 17, I had a vehicle licence and then bought a second-hand Toyota Land Cruiser with a horse crate on the back. I loaded up my two horses and two dogs and I was off to work for my first real employer at $20 a day, compared to $20 a week. I was in seventh heaven.

He was a tough man to work for and would knock you down with a stick if you gave him any backchat. I came close but I saw the error of my ways in a flash and agreed he was the one paying my wages and it was better doing it his way. Ted Colson was his name and I learned a thing or two from him before my time was through. He was a hard man but I learned the most valuable lesson of all my working life: the boss is always right. He wasn't big on hygiene either. He sent us off down to the creek for a bath and he'd say he'd be along right behind us. Of course, that never happened and I never saw him have a bogey the whole time I worked with him. He certainly wasn't keen on water.

I also worked up distaste for curry, all thanks to Ted. He would make up a big stew and leave it out on the stove. There it stayed, day after day. It never once was put in the fridge. It was an old kero fridge with a light that used to go out on the kero wick. This caused the fridge not to work properly. With no flame, the fridge was totally useless. Ted was not one for fixing the fridge, so the stew remained on the edge of the stove day in, day out, to the point where it started to go green, in other words, rotten.

Ted, not wanting to be one to waste the stew, plied it with loads of curry and the next day the treatment was the same until we got to a point we were drinking more black tea than eating curry. Ted wondered what was wrong with us. To this day, I'm not keen on curry, but we survived and never got food poisoning. We just got tougher.

These were carefree days in many ways. We got out of bed while it was still black and then off to get the horses in. Mind you, we took turns. Most days in summer, it was well over 100° and black tea seemed to have some magic ingredient. It would be dark by the time we unsaddled our horses and there was definitely no rush for the curried stew. We had the luxury though, of bathing in the creek. It was sheer luxury after long days in the saddle. Ted Coulson was our boss and he paid well. Greg South, my friend, and I were off to a flying start in the ringer department.

I also worked at home and at the same time secured a part-time job at the sale yards in Emerald, drafting cattle at night. I had two main horses that I rode at that time, one of them was part Arab/part thoroughbred. I called her Bonnie. She was near impossible to control and no one else wanted to ride her. She was wild and she knew it. When mustering, chasing cattle at full speed, she had one speed extra and that was overdrive. In those situations, I let her have her head and I learned just how to hold on. To try and pull up would more than likely end in disaster since she would be concentrating on the person trying to stop her with the reins instead of concentrating on where she was putting her feet.

The neighbour's son commented, "She'll kill him," that's how wild and out-of-control she was. She was rideable and I did ride her at my peril. I had some narrow escapes but the one that nearly brought me undone was while I was mustering some wild cattle. They were going as fast as they possibly could and she was going as fast as she possibly could. The next thing, down an embankment and into a creek we went. We submerged into the creek where there was a big log. She hit the log with her chest full on and catapulted me out of the saddle up onto her neck.

This day she must have been in partnership with the devil because in the blink of an eyelid, she was over the log, up the other embankment on her knees, and with one more blink of an eyelid, she was flat out again after the cattle. There was one minor problem. I was still up on her neck with my hands up near her head. It was absolutely no place to be riding a horse at full pace or any pace for that matter. Somehow, I got back down over the kneepads of the saddle and back into the saddle and continued with rounding up the cattle. That was the wildest ride mustering I'd ever encountered.

Most of the time spent mustering was simply going about our business with the horses walking. Through all the miles that I covered, it brought me a closer connection to the land and ultimately a closer connection to my Maker. I always felt connected to Him when I was out riding on a horse.

The only other spiritual influence in my life at the time was a book my dad gave me by Kahlil Gibran called *The Prophet;* an album (one you put on the record player) by Richard Harris called *There are too Many Saviours on my Cross;* and a play by Morris West that was on the radio called *The Heretic.*

The Richard Harris lines from that album I still carry with me today, "I am not orange, I am not green, I'm a half-ripe fruit needing both colours to grow and shame on you for having withered my orchard, shame, shame, shame."

I did spend most every other Sunday in church as a child, though this wasn't of my choosing. My main question for the preacher was if I was born a Chinese boy, grew up a good life, didn't commit any crimes, and treated those around me with kindness and compassion, would I still get to heaven?

He said, "No. You won't because you need to become a Christian." Well, it didn't take me long to work out I was with the wrong mob and it was even harder to get me into the church on a Sunday. At seven years of age, I seemed to have a depth of understanding beyond my years – a knowing. I also had a lot of trouble believing the streets were paved with gold in heaven. I couldn't see why you would need gold in heaven.

There was one story that really captured my heart from my childhood time in church. It was the story of Christ and St Peter walking on water. For me, Christ was showing me that it was possible to rematerialise or dematerialise my body. I spoke with a colleague and h confirmed that Christ could've used either of two methods to walk on water. I He suggested that one way Jesus could have used to walk on water, was that he may have made his body less dense than the water and, as a result, semi-materialised his physical body.

The shamans of many tribes around the world have been doing this for up to 60,000 years. While I'm still in the learning process, I have managed to achieve the same thing a few times. My work colleague, Daniel, has seen me on two occasions in two completely different places when it's seemingly not physically possible to be in two places at the same time.

He would say to me, "Here is the man that appears in two places at once." He would say it with other work colleagues present and I would kind of shrink off into the distance not wanting anyone to know too much about me. To be able to do this, it took me six years of quietening the mind through meditation via CDs and MP3 downloads which are the good works of Panayiota Theodoki-Atteshlis, daughter of Dr Stylianos Atteshlis.

When Jesus spoke of his miracles, he said, "All these things you shall do and more. Truly, truly, I say to you, whoever believes in me will also do the works that I do, and greater works than these will he do, because I am going to the Father." (John 14:12)

One Chinese proverb says, "The miracle is not to fly in the air or to walk on the water but to walk on the Earth."

The most accurate way to validate what happened on that day that Peter walked on water is to access what are called the Akashic Records. These are the records of everything and every event that has ever occurred on planet Earth. They can be accessed through meditation.

From the moment I heard the story of Christ walking on water as a child, I knew that one day I would attempt to do something similar. Being able to construct an elementa of myself has been a fulfilment of that long-held dream. The real accomplishment is quieting the mind; the other so-called miracles are just a by-product.

I do believe this is what Nicola Tesla was talking about when he uttered these words, "Everything is energy and that's all there is to it. Match the frequency of the reality you want and you cannot help but get that reality. It can be no other way. This is not philosophy. This is physics."

CHAPTER 2

MY FIRST AND SECOND VISIONS

When I was 18 years of age, my dad arrived home one afternoon with the news he had bought a cattle and farming property called "Old Gordon" near Capella in Central Queensland. He intimated that both my brother Andrew and I would work together on the property. It was suggested, though never spelled out clearly, that, eventually, I was going to buy the property from Dad while Andrew would get his chance later. In the meantime, and understandably, Andrew was not happy about the deal which he was being dealt Ultimately, 12 months later, our lives would change forever when a bullet pierced the night.

The property was 3500 acres and it was quite rundown. We had to put a lot of work into it just to get it in decent working order. We grew sorghum and sunflowers on the best agricultural land and we, also, raised cattle. When it came time for farming, we each worked a 12-hour shift each. After that, we pumped water, fixed fences, and attended to maintenance. We worked damn hard and when we had a break from work, my girlfriend used to come to visit. We'd spend two or three days together depending on her work roster. We decided on a short holiday. We headed to Townsville and then later to her sister's place. She sorted out her leave with her employers at the hospital, packed, and we were on our way.

We had travelled approximately 600km down Highway 1 and were probably 40 kilometres out of Townsville when I looked out of the passenger side window and saw this most amazing scene. It was as if one giant movie screen like those old drive-in movie screens multiplied by 20 had all joined. I didn't realise that at the time, but I was experiencing my first vision.

I knew I was driving the car and I could see this huge picture superimposed over the landscape. It was as real as real could be. It was like a massive movie screen and I had climbed into it, I was part of it. I was part of the movie. What I saw in this scene were my two favourite horses, my two dogs, and then there was my home: a caravan with a corrugated lean. There was a fire there with smoke rising and the billy was on to boil getting ready for a nice cuppa tea. I felt like I had entered heaven. This was complete oneness and the kind of oneness that mystics speak of. I was at one with everything physically and spiritually, all at the same time.

As I continued driving to Townsville, the vision was communicating to me to do a radio program, more specifically, a religious radio program and I was the broadcaster. I had never seen a radio transmitter, aerial, studio or even a microphone. I told my girlfriend what I'd seen but she wasn't able to interpret what had just transpired, since she didn't see what I saw. I drove on down the highway and didn't tell another soul for many years. We stayed with my girlfriend's sister for about a week and then returned home to our separate abodes.

Apart from experiencing a vision that I wasn't able to talk about with anybody, I arrived home only to find out Andrew never gave that important letter to Mum and Dad to let them know what I was doing. What was worse, nobody (and I mean nobody) in the whole family took up my cause. They let it all just ride by. It was just too complicated. I was, therefore, made to look like a total fool for having taken off with my girlfriend for some fun and games and not letting anybody know. I felt totally gutted and abandoned by my family. They didn't believe what happened the night that shot was fired.

I left the house and walked aimlessly until I found myself on the edge of a little dam, tears pouring down my cheek as I sang the words to a Kris Kristofferson's song. The lyrics I sang were, "Why me Lord, what have I ever done to deserve even one of the pleasures of known." Therefore, the chances of me discussing that vision with my family at that point were about 100 to 1, since they couldn't even trust me nor believe the reasons I had for going away. That was the end of it. I tucked it away in the far recesses of my mind never to be talked about again.

While visions and similar things were not talked about much in 1975, I've since found a group in 2016 called the Spiritual Emergency Network. They do research into visions, hearing voices, and other things. They found that nearly one in seven people hear voices, see visions, or have other forms of sensory experience that other people do not. Some research indicates that an overwhelming majority of people have some form of spiritual, mystical, or visionary experience during their lives.

SEN Australia Inc. is part of the international network that was founded by Christina Grof in 1980. The term "Spiritual Emergence" was first coined by Dr Stanislav and Christina Grof. They are therapists, researchers, and writers in the field of personal transformation.

I was 21, sitting right on top of the world in every department, lean as a kangaroo dog, and I didn't have an ounce of spare fat as I fitted 30" x 32" Levi's.

Then it happened, my world as I knew it was about to come undone. All in the space of a week, my world was turning to hell. We had a young mare called Lisa that had just been broken in and I had taken to working her. She was a little flighty but she trusted me, and this looked like the beginning of a great partnership. She had a beautiful mouth and she was fluid when she cantered. I'd only ever struck one horse like her before and she was the one I saw in the vision on the way to Townsville.

On this particular day, we were cantering along when Lisa started to buck for no apparent reason. She bucked so high and hard it was all over in seconds. The next thing I knew I was lying on the ground and couldn't move my legs. I must've been there 10 or 15 minutes before I could feel my back and legs. I got up, went to the horse at the back of the paddock, caught the horse again, girthed the saddle up tight, opened the gate out onto the big paddock, climbed on, urged her into a canter, then raked my two thumbs down the shoulders and said out loud, "If you want a buck, let's go." Well, she could barely get six inches off the ground. She knew I had her measure.

By nightfall, fluid from my spinal cord had swollen up under the skin on my back. The next thing I knew, I was in an ambulance on the way to Rockhampton Hospital. After intensive x-rays, it was ascertained I had Spondylolisthesis. I was actually born with it but, unlike Spina Bifida, I was still able to walk. The news was I would have to leave the land because, even if I had surgery like a bone graft, if I fell off a horse again it would break all around the bone graft. The orthopedic surgeon showed me the x-rays of my lower back and to this very day the fifth lumbar vertebrae is only millimetres away from my spinal cord. My understanding of Spondylolisthesis is that the forward displacement of a vertebra, especially the fifth lumbar vertebra, most commonly occurs after a fracture. It's as if someone got a knife and cut completely through the vertebrae that are normally one with the pelvis.

I didn't want to leave all I had dreamed of behind. The doctors devised a back brace for me to wear which was highly unsuccessful. I could no longer sit easy on a horse or do very heavy manual work. Not long after all of that, I was using Oxy Acetylene to build a grid to stop cattle getting out of their paddock when my most faithful friend of all, my cattle dog called Boxer, decided to go chase a fuel truck. He never chased a car or truck ever before in his life, yet somehow this day was different. It was over in seconds. He was my last best friend I had in the world at that moment.

It was my girlfriend, my back, and my dog: the trifecta. I decided that enough was enough. I went to town, bought a bottle of rum and drank it as quickly as I could. However, all I managed to do was get sick. I couldn't even get drunk.

One of the jobs I attended to was spraying some bags of wheat with a chemical spray to kill the weevils. The wheat was left over after we planted all that we needed to. I mixed the concoction up and trebled the dose for good measure. I was sure gonna give those little weevils their comeuppance. I had no protection over my nose or mouth, and went blindly ahead and sprayed.

Many hours later, my brother found me barely breathing and woke me up. I had nearly poisoned myself with the weevil spray. The exact damage I did to my brain I will probably never know. However, it showed up very strongly in a hair sample that a medical specialist sent to Boulder, Colorado in the US.

Dad decided it would be better for me to work the property on my own after having bought bigger more expensive machinery. It was big enough so one man could do the work of two. All of that was going okay until I got to the point where I was having trouble moving my legs and getting out of bed in the morning. There some mornings that I was partly paralysed and in total fear that I would never walk again. I didn't want to tell anyone in the family because I felt like a failure. I really had put all of my eggs in one basket.

The numbness in my legs grew worse. I was lying in bed longer with no feeling in them. I couldn't even get up to make a phone call. The spondylolisthesis was wreaking havoc on my life. Anyway, decision time was due and I had to walk away from everything I held dear. I walked down the front steps of that house with tears in my eyes and with no idea of where to go next.

Much later in life, I came across these words from John Steinbeck from his book *The Grapes of Wrath* where he says, "If a man needs 1 million acres to make him feel rich, seems to me he needs it 'course he feels awful poor inside his self, and if he's poor in himself, there ain't no million acres gunna make him feel rich, and maybe he is disappointed that nothing he can do will make him feel rich." It took a big chunk of life to understand what Steinbeck was talking about. At the moment, I was about as wiped out as a man can get. I was the man that felt he needed one million acres to make him feel rich.

My dad suggested that I take on a job with a firm called Dalgety's. They were stock and station agents dealing with people who had farms and cattle properties. I tried but to be truthful, I really wasn't interested. Why? Why did it happen to me? I must have asked that question a 1000 times and I never ever could come up with a half-decent answer. I started drinking, getting very interested in the opposite sex, and started on an even deeper downhill slide, not caring about the consequences of my actions. I didn't really care if I lived or died and that's exactly what nearly transpired next.

I was still working at Dalgety's. I was driving home on a Friday afternoon after lunch to attend my sister's wedding since I was to be best man. I still haven't figured it out to this day, but somewhere between Biloela and Wowan either a mechanical fault occurred or I went to sleep at the wheel of the car. As a result, the car veered to the left of the highway and broke off a telecom poll. Since I didn't have the seat belt on, I went through the windscreen of the car and landed approximately 30m from where the car had come to a standstill. All the doors were still closed and the windscreen shattered so the ambulance guys passed on their reading of the situation that I was flung out like a wrecking ball through the windscreen.

The Telecom crew from Rockhampton found me unconscious and lying in the hot sun. They may not have found me for quite some time if I hadn't taken out the telecom poll that was pivotal in telephone communication between Biloela and Rockhampton. I crashed sometime after lunch. The telecom crew came looking for the disruption in telecommunications. They found the busted pole completely broken off the ground, a white Falcon on its side, and Greg Reid about 30m from the car.

All I can remember is being put into the ambulance and seeing the white car on the side in the distance. They wouldn't let me drink because I had been in the sun too long. All I got was an ice cube to suck on while they taxied me to Rockhampton.

Looking back, I was one very lucky person. When they found me, my right leg was at a right angle to my knee. Both my ACLs were broken; I had a broken collarbone, and minor internal injuries. Because they didn't have the technology they have now, the doctor had to improvise and stitch ligaments from the left side of my right leg on the front of the knee and repair the right ligament that went down the outside.

The area where the doctor had operated on the knee, became infected and pushed up against the Plaster of Paris encasing my right leg. The morphine stopped working because the pain was so intense but I couldn't get anybody to listen to me so I embarked on another strategy. I saved up a couple of sleeping pills and took them with the morphine shot. I then managed to fall out of bed, knocking over the little bedside table and cracking the plaster. I ended up under the bed and wouldn't come out until somebody gave me a cigarette. I hadn't had a smoke in weeks. Well, the good news was I had to get a new plaster on. That's when the doctor discovered the infection and the pain I'd been in for the past three weeks.

My overall hospital stay was about 6 months. It was a total of 12 months before I was walking without crutches. Upon my release from the hospital, I started some serious party going. My friends would pick me up while I was still on crutches and take me off to the nearest party. I soon developed the new skill of being the life of the party. It seemed that if heaven didn't want me, I'd make my own way to hell.

Among all this newfound freedom with drinking and girls, I thought I'd found a place for me. It might have stayed that way, if it hadn't been for the intervention of my sister. I was lying on the bed recovering after a big night out when she came to interrupt my interlude. She wanted to know what I was doing with my life and I just replied, "I'm having a good time." Words were exchanged between us. However, in the end, I told her about the vision I had way back when I was 21 on my way to Townsville.

She said, "Well, you're a stupid idiot; can't you see that God is talking to you?" She knew I'd never seen a radio studio, a radio transmitter site, and a radio aerial, not even a radio announcer and here she was advocating on behalf of God to take up a career in broadcasting.

That's exactly what I embarked upon. I went to 4RO Rockhampton to do a voice test. This soon followed with an application for a job in Gladstone even though I had no previous experience.

After some research, I decided to go to radio school at 4BH in Brisbane. However, the only problem was that I had to find a job to pay the rent to feed myself and get myself through radio school. Can you imagine the culture shock of someone having lived all his life in the country or in a small town, moving to a large city like Brisbane? I got a job working in the big sale yards where they sold cattle at Cannon Hill. At the time, they were the biggest yards in Queensland.

The bad news came from my radio tutor, when he informed me that I spoke with a nasal, western drawl. He said that I had to learn to speak properly if I was ever to get a job in radio. Therefore, while I walked between the pens of cattle where I worked at Cannon Hill, I recited poetry, Shakespeare, anything at all, learning to speak the way broadcasters spoke with a deep voice back in the 70s. These days anything goes. However, I learned many valuable things that I still hold dear today. One of those things is that communication really is from the heart and not the head.

It's one thing going to radio school, it's quite another finding a radio job. I embarked on a road trip from Central Queensland right down the east coast of Australia. I called on every radio station that I could find along the way. I dropped off my audition cassettes and prayed that one day that telephone call would come. I found myself losing my way again and losing faith because 12 months went by and I still didn't have my dream job. In a big city like Brisbane, there were so many distractions, nightclubs, alcohol, girls, and friends turning up from my hometown looking for someone to take them out on a good time. I was just repeating the same mistakes I'd made after I got out of the hospital. The only difference was the town.

I decided to leave Brisbane for a few months and head bush for a while out to my brother-in-law and sister's place at Dirrinbandi. Nev, my brother-in-law, said he had some work for me and would repay in kind with board and food. For the moment, that was all I needed: some good hard work, plenty of sweat, and to totally forget about a career in radio for a while. I worked mustering sheep with him, fencing, and I agreed to help him break in some horses (tame them), if he would ride them at the end of the process because of my bad back. I couldn't afford to take a bad fall and spend the rest of my days in wheelchair. We worked on the horses in the round yard over the period of two weeks and got them to the point where they were tame enough to ride. I kind-of guessed it in the back of my mind that he was going to ask me to ride them.

I agreed and took the first horse out in the company of an older, educated mare and everything went according to plan. My brother-in-law rode the older horse and I rode the young one. It came time for the one that looked a bit livelier and we left the yard in the company of the older horse that Nev was on. Once again, everything was going according to plan until his kelpie dog appeared on the scene and started barking right behind the young mare that I was on. She took fright and was quickly into a canter. The dog followed, barking all the while. When the mare went faster, the dog got faster. The mare was now at a flat gallop and we just approached some very unhospitable country to travel through.

Neither the mare nor the dog slowed down. We were travelling through what is called a lignum scrub, which is a place that only wild pigs inhabit. We kept up this pace until the mare ran out of puff and the dog was there with tongue hanging out looking for a bravery award. I was actually the one that should have had the bravery award. It was one of the wildest rides I have ever had in my life. To this day, I don't know what kept me in the saddle.

When Nev arrived at the scene, he was having trouble keeping himself from laughing. I was having trouble keeping myself from getting angry because I wasn't seeing the funny side of things at all. It could be said the mare was officially broken in at that stage, since she was now rideable. I helped him with sheep shearing, using a manual wool press, but with my crook back that didn't last for long either.

Nev owned a .357 Magnum that I got to use on the back of a horse chasing wild pigs. It wasn't like the movies at all. The pigs were very hard to hit because the pistol was going up and down in movement with the horse. However, it had been one of my lifelong dreams to do such a thing and I was glad I accomplished it, even if it wasn't like I had imagined. His property was next door to Cubby Station that now claims to be the largest cotton farm in Australia.

We had many memorable moments in the six months I stayed with my brother-in-law and sister. One of those moments was rescuing sheep from rising floodwaters and physically making them swim across a flooded creek so they get to safe ground on the other side. I can tell you that when a sheep doesn't want to swim a flooded creek, he really doesn't want to. It must've taken the best part of one day to get just one mob across this creek. At the end of the day, exhausted and soaking wet, we headed for home with the sheep safe and the job completed.

I stayed approximately six months with Nev and Del. During that time, I started to learn to play the guitar, write songs and write a couple of my very first poems. I had some memorable times there just working for my tucker. I went back to Brisbane to reactivate the idea of becoming a radio broadcaster, checking the industry magazines, making some phone calls and looking for that job.

The good Lord must have figured that I still had some positive karma in my account because that phone call I'd waited for so long eventually came. It came from Betty Corbett from 4ZR Roma, inquiring if I could come for an interview. Within 24 hours, I was in her office in Roma and, before I left, I had the job. Roma is about a 5½-hour trip, approximately 500km west of Brisbane. I managed to get some share accommodation with a fellow broadcaster from the radio station, Mike Stewart. I still stay in touch with him as our paths have crossed numerous times over the years.

The joy of finally having my dream come true turned a touch sour a week after I started at 4ZR. I went out to a friend's place for dinner and, while travelling back home in the dark on a road I didn't know very well, the car spun out into a corner. It hit one of the large posts that made up a grid. These grids typically had steel railings welded about 4 inches apart that the cars travelled over. Cattle fencing was attached to these large posts. The whole idea was that the cattle wouldn't put their feet on the steel railings because there were gaps in them and most cattle preferred something much more secure to walk across. The grids were designed to allow cars to pass over without having to get out to open and shut the gate. They were meant to keep cattle separated from one side of the fence to the other. My car was sitting pretty much on top of this large post with a massive dent in the middle of it. Luckily, other travelers using the road spotted the accident and took me to Roma Hospital. All the teeth on the top of the right-hand side of my mouth were broken off at the roots. Upon my release from the hospital a week later, I went back to work with five teeth missing. I had to go to the dentist to get the roots extracted so I could have a plate. Once a week for five weeks, I went to the dentist to get another tooth extracted. Meanwhile, I was doing my best to talk while on the radio with missing five teeth. It took a bit over two months to have the teeth extracted and a plate made up to replace them.

What a joy it was the day when my false teeth arrived. I could actually talk properly. and it was from that point on that my radio career really began. I was doing the drive-time shift. I turned it into something full of fun, yet bordering on a bit out there. Whatever the magic ingredient was, it was working and people were turning back to the station that hadn't had active listeners for years. I took it to the very edge of what was acceptable and my poor manager was on cyclone alert every time I was on air.

One day, the radio station technician sided with me, while I recorded a very poor tasteless joke. We hatched a plan that when I would normally read the weather, I would do this joke. The trick was that I would actually say an acceptable joke live on air while the technician played the inappropriate version over the monitor system that went right into the office of the manager. At the time, she had a client, so she was half listening to the client and half listening to some offending words coming across the speaker.

In the end, it was too much for her. She left the client in the office and came looking for me. I had vacated the studio sensing trouble, only to find out from one of my fellow broadcasters that she'd said, "When you find him, tell him he's sacked." It was with much trepidation that I approached my manager the following day. The technician had told her it was just a joke, but she still wasn't seeing the funny side. I remained employed nearly 12 months at 4ZR and my manager didn't see the funny side of that joke right up until the day I left.

I later applied for a position as a Breakfast Announcer at 4KZ Innisfail, North Queensland over 1,270km north of Roma. I was successful with my application. There was one of the biggest going-away parties that Roma had seen for a long time. I drove my little van with not too much in my head until I reached a place near Innisfail called Tully. Just out of Tully, I looked up and saw the rainforest on my right-hand side and I said to myself, "I've been here before." As my journey began to unfold, this place would be one of many that I would have visited in the North. I felt a strong sense of déjà vu.

I hosted the breakfast program on 4KZ for about 12 months and then management moved me into the morning program that ran from 9 AM to 1 PM. This new timeslot was a much quieter format of music that had a calming effect on me. I abandoned the manic approach that I had employed at 4KR in Roma. I began building a new on-air persona. This one had a subtle spiritual component. I began reading poetry on air and I would finish my radio program with a "Thought for the day."

Listeners began to call, write letters, and occasionally would personally drop in at the studios to say hello. I knew that I had a winning formula. As a result, management asked me if I wanted to become Program Director. It took me 2.5 seconds to consider and the job was mine. Slowly, but surely I moved the sound of the station away from a purely top-40 station to one where the lyrics of a song became important.

One weekend at a place call Murray Falls, I went with a few friends to experience some new places in North Queensland. We swam at the Falls, had lunch and then swam some more. On my way back up the walkway to our picnic table, after another swim, I glanced off to my left and saw about 15 Aboriginal people standing and looking at me. There's nothing wrong with 15 Aboriginal people looking at me. That was not a problem. The problem was that I realised they were not of this world. They were of the **a**stral world or as Aborigines say, "The Dreamtime." They made no signals to me. They just stood and looked at me.

Our family has no indigenous bloodlines from the past. I had no specific connection with indigenous people apart from having spent my childhood growing up with them. What did 15 indigenous spirit people want with me? Just like my first vision, I didn't tell a soul. I just carried on as if nothing had happened. Nearly 20 years would pass before I would again see Aboriginal people in the spirit/astral world. All this time I remained fully employed and for the most part, employed as a radio announcer.

I entered the Pater Radio Awards while program director at 4KZ. The first year I entered, they were hosted in Sydney and I reached the finals of the most creative music programmer in provincial Australia. The following year, I entered the same awards competition again but this time I entered in the category for Most Creative Music Programmer in all of Australia, including the capital cities. I made the finals once again and on that night, the host of the awards singled me out and said, " . . . represented all the awards stood for." The Prime Minister at the time was Bob Hawke and he mentioned me in his address stating that I was an example of what the awards stood for.

I was also recognised as a Program Director who was breaking new songs. This means someone who would take a risk to play a song by a band that no one else was playing on the radio. This happened with the band call "Foster and Allen" and a song called "When You Were Sweet 16." The record company representative had communication with the band to let them know that I was the first Program Director in Australia to break their song. They asked the record company representative to pass on to me an invitation that if ever I were to come to Ireland, I would have a place to stay with any of the band members.

I also met my wife in Innisfail. We were married in a Greek Church in 1981. My ancestors were English, Irish, Scottish, French and German, but my upbringing was English. Therefore, to be exposed to another culture, was totally out of my depth. My first meeting with her parents was at the first dinner at their house. The main course was stewed octopus in red wine. I was quite sure it that would make me sick so I sat close to the outside door. I got the shock of my life when I found how delicious it was. I later learned to cook this unique dish myself. I also acquired a taste for many other Greek foods.

Our first son was born in Innisfail in 1983. We named him Clinton. It was also in the Innisfail area that I started doing discos. This was a personal venture separate from my work at the radio station. I earned a reputation for being able to attract a big crowd. When I worked on Friday and Saturday nights, I could earn more money than what I earned a week at the radio station. It was good but it still wasn't what I was looking for. What I was looking for found me. I wasn't exactly ready for it, even though at a subconscious level, I was craving the experience.

In 1984, I accepted an offer to become Program Director/ Morning Announcer at 2QN in New South Wales at Deniliquin right on the Edward River and not far from the Murray River. It seemed like it was going to be a better job with better pay and more responsibility.

Our second baby was born there and I was present at the birth. We named him Sean. He was a placid child but he used to get wind and a pain in the tummy after he'd been fed. I observed that if I put him in a stroller and pushed him around the neighbourhood, his wind would break and he'd be happy once more. The trick was to engage in winter mornings in Deniliquin that was somewhere around -5°. I pushed him nearly every other morning down those freezing streets. Sean was all rugged up with just his tiny little face poking out in the pram. We shared some special time in those mornings and I've got them securely filed away forever in a special memory department in my mind.

I also had the opportunity to experience talkback radio for the first time. I saw this strange equipment that I'd never seen before in the rack in the technical room at the radio station and I asked the technician what it was used for. He explained it was a "delay system" and gave me a rundown on how it operated technically and how to operate it. What it did, in effect, was to stretch out the program by seven seconds and that allowed the operator seven seconds in which to cut that part of the program out that had yet to go to air. In fact, the listeners were listening to a program that was delayed by seven seconds. This was a legal requirement to own and operate a delay system if they were doing talkback radio. By being able to dump part of the program, it safeguarded the radio station from legal matters like defamation and having undesirable swear words going to air.

In the 1970s and 1980s, swear words were deemed to be offensive and if a caller used a swear word while engaging with the station during talkback, a telephone interview or a live interview, then the station was deemed culpable for allowing this offensive material to go to air. If these protocols were breached, the Broadcasting Tribunal had the power to ask the owners of the station to relinquish their license to broadcast. I don't recall this ever happening but that power was still there. Every station I knew that had talkback radio as a part of their format, engaged a delay system in getting that program content to air.

Our technician at the time was one of the most engaging people I ever had the pleasure to meet. He had been at the top of his trade in Melbourne and now had a block of land near Deniliquin. He worked part-time at the station. In the relatively short time that I knew him, I observed the way of a simple man, someone who didn't want for much at all. He was my guiding light during my stay in Southern New South Wales. He gave me a book about radio, *The Magic Spark* and somehow, intuitively, I received the contents without ever reading it.

This was in the era when talkback radio was at its peak, with broadcasters like John laws and Darren Hinch. I made a promise to myself to develop my own style and not try to mimic what they were doing, even though they were the kings of the airwaves at the time. In consultation with management, I was given the go-ahead to do a talkback program on a Sunday night with the local Baptist minister. I took to the concept like a duck to water and soon had under my wings six months valuable talkback radio experience. We had a wide variety of guests. One man, in particular, stands out in my mind. He was the first person to rob a TAB betting agency just after they had installed new security measures. He simply leapt over the top of the newly installed partitioning walls and made off with the money. He eventually slipped up and was caught. He spent quite a bit of time in jail and it was during this time he found Christ.

Meanwhile, I started to become restless within myself. One night, while walking down a hallway that had no windows, I saw six squares of pure light each approximately 10" x 10". There was absolutely no way light could get in. At least, that's what I thought. I went up and back half a dozen times passing through where I expected the source of the light would have come from, expecting a shadow to appear at least on one wall. I walked past the six squares repeatedly, hoping that a shadow would be cast. It seemed to me the light was just manifesting on its own. This was a light form that I'd never seen before; it was so pure, so soft that I had an urge to go into the *source* of the light and be transported to another dimension.

I didn't know what to do next. Was this a message from some foreign source? What was I supposed to do? These questions lay heavy on my mind for the next three months and still I didn't get any answer. I have heard that these kinds of things that happen in the Bible seem to be much simpler and easier for the recipient to understand. Well, it looked like I wasn't going get it the easy way. The answer seemed to be just under the surface waiting for me to understand.

At the same time, while I was trying to understand the six squares of light, I started lying back in my lazy boy chair, closing my eyes and controlling my breath so it went longer and deeper. I found that in breathing this way, I could slow down my mind. I didn't learn this technique from a book or discover it from any other source, it just came naturally. I later came to understand that what I was doing was meditating. However, the deep breathing I was doing had a twist to it. I had this feeling I'd used this technique in a faraway land in a previous incarnation. It just came so easy to me that I thought everyone did this.

I would breathe in, get my breath and then go deeper, deeper, and slower. In my mind, I would then hold both of my arms out and slowly lift them up and down. Eventually, I would go out of my body. If I failed in my concentration and breathing, I fell back to earth and into my body. I would then do it all over again. I was quite aware that I was thousands of feet off the ground. I was just like a bird. I'd use my arms like wings and fly over vast tracts of country. I could see in considerable detail what was happening on the ground, trees, and rivers, fields of produce, other birds and animals. I say other birds because at this point, when I left my body, I became an eagle. I would fly like this for between 15 or 20 minutes.

Some people are aware that meditation is beneficial. It helps to reduce stress, depression, anxiety, blood pressure, and has many other benefits. While, at the time, I was oblivious to all of that, I would in the years to come understand that regular meditation has long-term effects. It is believed that it can transform your brain structure, create new circuits or change the way neurons talk to each other.

Squares of white light, out-of-body experiences, rides on an outlaw grey mare and trouble sleeping at night, made me feel like I didn't belong in Deniliquin anymore. I ended up saying to my wife, "How about we head back to North Queensland. I can't stand one more winter in this place." The first thing my wife said was, "You haven't got a job." I was well aware I was about to resign my present position and head north into the unknown. The six squares of light were finally starting to reveal their message. I was to return to North Queensland but what I was to do when I got there, was unknown to me.

I had quite a few sleepless nights mulling over my decision to quit my job and head back north. On one of these sleepless nights, I was wide awake and up around 1 AM. The house we were renting backed onto a two acre vacant lot. A grey horse was the chief resident of those acres. However, she had a real attitude problem. She bit anyone who went near her (except the girl that used to ride her). I had this feeling that a spiritual force was guiding me on my path and I was just beginning to listen to this guiding light within.

On this particular night, I felt that the light was on inside. I went up to this horse at the back gate and started talking to her. I felt brave enough to open the gate and go into her paddock. I kept talking to her, rubbing her neck with my hand, and then I grabbed hold of her mane and jumped from the ground right onto her back. She didn't buck or race off in fright, so I dug my heels into her ribs then guided her with my legs and away we went into the beautiful moonlit night. I rode her for about 10 minutes, guided her to our back gate and slid off.

There I was at 1 AM in the morning on top of this horse that used to monster anybody that went near her, apart from a regular rider. I had no bridle and reins to guide her and no saddle to keep me from falling off. The message that the author of those six squares had for me was starting to sink in. This was several years before I had given my life to Christ. Even though I knew that something of a spiritual nature was happening within me, I was wary of using the name Christ. I tried unsuccessfully to describe the six white squares to my wife and seeing that I was having trouble deciphering them, I decided the best policy was to keep quiet about what I had witnessed.

Within weeks, I had another vision and this time I saw a white pyramid. I was told that I would find it in North Queensland. Based on this limited information, I made my decision and handed in my resignation, even though my manager tried unsuccessfully to get me to stay. I bought a tandem trailer with mesh sides and loaded it with all of our worldly possessions. One loaded trailer included: my wife, our two sons, a dog, and me. The journey of 2000km that lay in front of us, had this feeling of Moses heading back to the Promised Land. The dog was the biggest mistake. She kept lying on the children and they complained throughout the trip. "The dog is laying on me," was the refrain. I started to get a picture of a white pyramid while I was driving. One more to add to the list of "I don't know what that means."

We arrived safe and sound back in the township of Innisfail. Within a couple of weeks, I secured a job as a salesman working for the radio station I used to work for four years earlier, 4KZ. This was a new challenge to me, as I'd never held a sales position before.

Within 12 months, I was the number one salesman on the team. I had the added advantage of having worked for nearly 10 years as a radio broadcaster and, in that time, I had voiced many commercials. As a result, I was able to write good copy and bring it to life in a 30-second ad. What was also of great benefit to me and to the businesses that I represented, was that the majority of the ads I wrote and voiced were working. Businesses were seeing a direct link between the sales in their shops and the commercials I was writing and voicing. Stock was going out the door. They were then keen to buy more advertising and so the wheel of commerce went around and around.

I was now taking home a good wage and a very good commission on top of it. I also had a deal worked out with a local hotel where they supplied my boss and me a large amount of alcohol in bonuses each month for the results that I was achieving. They were making money and they were happy to share in the spoils. There was all that alcohol and it was free. My thirst grew larger every day. I drank to excess just because it was there. I couldn't see that I was going backwards down a one-way track. We moved from Innisfail to a beachside town called Kurramine Beach. It was about 40 km south of Innisfail. I travelled the 40 km to and from work every day.

My battle with the bottle was having a detrimental effect on my marriage, even though I couldn't see it at the time. The strangest thing then happened as I started to have a spiritual awakening. Some people call it a spiritual emergence. Others call it a spiritual emergency. I didn't know what to call it. I'd never experienced anything else like it before in my life. The most honest description I can give to this experience is that of a *spiritual awakening*. I was having trouble sleeping. In order to counter that, I started walking kilometre after kilometre on the beach at night. I had no specific purpose. I just walked and walked. I would get home a couple of hours later, grab some sleep and off to work I would go. I kept this up for about six months and I became at one with the night. I would swim in crocodile-infested creeks and slowly, but surely, I started to enter the spirit world known, also, as the astral world; others call it the psychical world, and still others the Dreamtime.

The truth of the matter is I didn't know what world I was in. I'd never been in these worlds before and I didn't have a mentor or guide to help me get out and back into what we know as the third dimension, Mother Earth. All I knew was I had a profound sense that Jesus was with me. I didn't know what he wanted if, indeed, he wanted anything. I just knew that something was about to happen. One night, I experienced my first out-of-body incident (perhaps it was time travel).

I travelled back in time to the night when Jesus was in the garden of Gethsemane just before the crucifixion. This time I wasn't looking in, I was at the scene. Christ was about 100 yards in front of where I was. The Roman soldiers were heading toward him and some of the disciples. The soldiers were carrying lights (the ones on the end of a stick). Even though there was light from the soldiers' lamps, the night seemed blacker than black. Although Christ had told the disciples of his fate, nobody really believed it was going to happen. When the soldiers came with their lights, most people gathered in the garden fell into a state of shock. How did I witness such an event? It was because of the fact that in a past incarnation, I was actually in the garden of Gethsemane on the night Judas betrayed Christ with a kiss on the cheek.

Edgar Cayce explains the Akashic Records this way, "It is this system that acts as the central storehouse of all information for every individual who has ever lived upon the earth. More than just a reservoir of events, the Akashic Records contain every deed, word, feeling, thought, and intent that has ever occurred at any time in the history of the world." Other people refer to the Akashic Records as the Cosmic Consciousness. Carl Jung used this term to describe the phenomena.

I was also well aware of where I was in the real world. I was not far from the boat ramp, and in among the trees near the local shop. I was able to be in both realities at the same time and while I was in this state, I raised both arms to the heavens and said, "Christ, I give my life to you."

While the Akashic Records are the past, the astral plane is the fourth dimension with its many distinct planes. I accessed the astral plane a number of times during this period. One particular time, I was able to journey to a place that resembled heaven. It simply defies description because everything was so different. I could summon a horse just by calling out his name and he would come. There were slip rails but they weren't needed because the horses in that realm were free. When I called one, it would come to me in a split second and when I rode the horse, we didn't need a bridle or saddle. I just hung onto his mane and we went through the air. In this dimension, everything becomes what you think. If you think it, it becomes your reality. If you want a mansion, you've got it. Although given time, most people will realise they don't need a house at all. They don't even need to sleep.

I spent the next six months slipping in and out of this altered state of consciousness. I did this while keeping down a full-time job and helping to raise a family. The three boys and I found camping to be something that we all enjoyed. We camped at nearly every available camping spot in North Queensland. Their mother wasn't keen on camping and stayed home.

We would drag the net for bait at the beach and use an old disused net to catch fish, crabs and even a stingray. We'd cook damper in the camp oven and the boys would use the damper mix to put on the end of a stick and slowly turn it on the fire to have their own little mini dampers, and out would come the butter and syrup.

They were all mad keen on the water, too. If we weren't camping most times, we would be in a swimming hole somewhere in North Queensland. It didn't seem to matter if it was summer or winter, those boys just loved the water.

On the outside, I was doing my best to keep it all together. However, on the inside, I was crying out for a teacher, guide or anyone who had experienced the kinds of things that happened to me in the last 12 months.

My first teacher came unexpectedly. His name was David Mowaljarlai and he had written a book called *Yorro Yorro*. He was the first man who was able to bring some clarity to my journey toward self-realisation. He was an Aboriginal man of the Ngarinyin language, a Law man from Mowanjum near Derby, WA Australia. I wrote to ask him to teach me to be a Banman (a healer). First, he replied by telephone. I was working at the *Innisfail Advocate* at the time and I can still recall his words very clearly. He said, "You want to be a Banman, just know that you are already. The Wandjinas (spirit beings) have come to you." At this point, I'd love to share with you a letter David wrote to me in 1996.

> *Dear Greg,*
>
> *Your excitement of discovery of yourself is greatly acknowledged and understood. A Banman in themselves is born with a gift and nurtured in life to develop their knowledge by the Teacher of life. The different stages of initiations is always personal and with the spirit itself. Once one has found the stillness inside the ego dies the thing that separates one from the source. There is no need to identify that "I am this… Just I am."*
>
> *There is no more convincing others who and what one is. Once a master recognises that they always had been "the one", then everything stops. The story begins and ends there.*
>
> *Everyone on this planet has this knowledge and how they choose to acknowledge it, well that's a different story, yet to say. You have asked for a teacher and know that it is already.*
>
> *The water under the sand is right where you are. Trust is the key. Trust always in your own instincts without having to have outside confirmation. Trust in yourself*

as there is no other. Know that our hearts are with you in your journey and we acknowledge you. David and Michelle.

I treasure the letter and the phone call. In fact, I still have a copy of the letter today. I spent many years unraveling the contents of the letter. I have read it many times over until I finally found the "I am" that lay within. David passed away in September. I'd only just come to know him and he was gone. In the following 48 hours, I wrote a poem about him and his life. I sent it off to the Kamali Land Council in Derby.

David

*I heard him speaking from
    Paris,
Just a few short weeks ago,
Explaining to those who didn't
    understand
what those famous paintings
    mean,
And on which path we should
    go.*

*He gave not only of himself,
He shared with us the richest
    civilization
this world has ever seen,
God asked him to smash the
    barriers,
And share with us his dream.*

Just a man in an Akubra hat,

*A king in a world becoming
    spiritually poor,
He never questioned the road
    he had to travel,
He never asked what for.*

*He knew deep within he had a
    mission to accomplish,
To hold onto those sacred ways,
A message for black and white,
Or numbered are our days.*

*I heard his message,
I'll hold it forever sacred in my
    heart,
I'll hold it and treasure it till
    comes the time,
When black and white are
    forced to make a new start.*

He taught me about the
    Wunggud,
Woodu time, Lejmorro, till now
    they're a part of me,
He taught me how to seek
    change without hatred,
And how oppression will finally
    set you free.

He taught us all to live and love,
And how to hold your head up
    high,
I hope to meet him in the big
    camp soon,
But in the meantime I'll just cry.

He had a traditional funeral in Derby. They read the lines of this poem as they wheeled the coffin into the church. The whole event was recorded as a documentary and later replayed on SBS television. Since it was a traditional funeral, the first one in 40 years, they took him in the coffin to a special place via helicopter. At the site, they took him out of the coffin, covered him in stone and stayed with him for three nights.

Eighteen months would pass until his countrymen returned to put his bones in a sacred place in a cave with his skull facing East. This is because the Ngarinyin nation, along with two other nations, believe that's where the power comes from. His influence on my life still lives with me today and I'm looking forward to that meeting I will have with him on the other side.

The Wandjina referred to by David are the great so-called higher intelligences that express themselves as the archangels within all the archangelic orders known and unknown to man.

They fit perfectly with the description Daskalos gave when talking of these so-called higher intelligences. Daskalos referred to these innumerable spirit beings that have never been born and will never die; they're eternal. Through spiritual discipline, we can come in conscious communication with these great intelligences. They rejoice in seeing us make our long awaited approach. They welcome us and are ready to reveal their great wisdom to any sincere seekers.

David Mowaljarlai's letter of August 1996 was to be the turning point in my life for me spiritually. Take away the veil of what we call reality and you step into a world the Aboriginal people of Australia call the Dreamtime - the world we visit in dreams. We do it every night, even if we don't recall the experience. We can also access this world while awake. For some it's easy while others can take years and even lifetimes to master.

It's all about frequency and vibrating at a certain frequency. Vibrate at that frequency and you can step into the spirit world. That's probably the easiest part; knowing how to get back out, that's a bit harder to learn. Anyone wishing to see what lies beyond the veil is encouraged to practise meditation and anything that stills the mind without the use of drugs or alcohol.

Einstein is attributed to saying, "Everything is energy and that's all there is to it." Match the frequency of the reality you want and you cannot help but get into that reality. So it is with these other worlds beyond the third dimension that we call Earth. Edgar Cayce puts it this way, "All manifestation of life is spirit. Hence matter, materiality, should be nothing. But when spirit is manifesting in a three-dimensional world of matter, form and spirit, it becomes subject to the laws of materiality, which in themselves are temporal, and thus subject to decay." (Cayce Reading 1678-1)

I was still living a double life. Most nights, I would get out of bed and walk the beach, searching for something and for whom I really was. I didn't know it at the time, but I'd taken the first tentative steps on the path to self-realisation.

I faced a number of mental health challenges yet I felt that an inner voice was directing my steps. My feet found the pathway that led to the door of the astral realms. In this altered state of consciousness, I found that I had the ability to explore and maneuver through other worlds in a moment and bring information back from the other multidimensional realities in a split second.

The Aboriginal people of Australia call these realms Dreamtime because they believe that's where you go when you dream. They also believe that you go to the same place when you die. I had asked David Mowaljarlai to teach me to be a healer back in August 1986, and now I stood at the threshold knowing that I had to heal myself first.

The altered states of consciousness came and went. They were like a new car that I was learning how to drive and I was having difficulty passing my learner's test. Richard Gordon once said, "A healer is someone who was sick and got well and a great healer is someone who got very sick and got well quickly." On the other hand, you could look at it this way, Joseph Campbell said, "The mystic is swimming in the same water the psychotic is drowning in."

Christ explained it best of all when he said, "If I told you earthly things and you do not believe, how will you believe if I tell you heavenly things?" That's exactly how I felt. There was no one other than David Mowaljarlai who I could confide in and he lived 3000 km on the other side of Australia. My sum total communication with him had been one phone call and one letter. However, that was some of the most important information I would ever receive.

Here I was with the biggest story of my life. It was the greatest gift that I'd been given thus far. However, I didn't know where to go or who to seek. I, therefore, started to read. I voraciously read anything on spirituality that I could get my hands on. I even went to the trouble of ordering two special books out of the library in Brisbane, *The Philosopher's Stone* and *Hermes Trismegistus*. However, none of it connected with what was deep inside of me.

From as long as I can remember, I've always had a feeling that I came from an Aboriginal background. Our family trees have been traced and no one can find an ounce of evidence to support my theory. As time went on, I learned about reincarnation and have since, through out-of-body experiences and other states of altered consciousness, found that I've been an Aboriginal man at least six times and an Aboriginal woman at least twice in the country they now call Australia. I have been able to identify nearly all of the places and all of the tribes that I once belonged to and still do, because that connection is never lost.

My eldest son, Clinton, witnessed one such experience. We were camped on the campground call Henrietta Creek in North Queensland. I had for some time been trying to get into a ceremonial ground called the Tchuken Bora Ground. The attraction for me was a tree that had been carved in the shape of the cassowary that was on the edge of the Bora Ground. It was carved in recognition of King Billy Cassowary, who was the last of a long line of warriors who tried to repel the White invasion. He dressed up in his war paint and regaled himself with cassowary feathers, slipping into the night to do whatever he could to keep him connected to his country.

I asked around and got the necessary permission to go on that country to find that famous Bora Ground. I made a couple of attempts nearly getting lost. Being the bushman that I was, I don't say that lightly. I went into that jungle with someone who grew up in that country as a small child and lived many years with his uncle. Therefore, if anybody was going to find the Bora Ground it was was going to be him. I'm not sure what forces were working against us, but even he got lost and we had to abandon the trip.

That only made me more determined to find this Bora Ground once and for all. I now had maps and a compass. I picked a month that wasn't too hot and early one morning finally headed off to track down this elusive Bora Ground. Halfway through the day, both of our compasses went on the blink, but we soldiered on. We eventually got to what I believe was the outside of the Bora Ground and found some very old empty beer bottles. That all fits with having found the Bora Ground, because at one stage there was a hotel built on it. Light was starting to fade and I had a decision to make. Do I go further or do I head for home? It was easy to get lost in the jungle once the sun had gone from view. I chose Clinton's safety ahead of my quest to find what King Billy had left behind.

On the way back, we noticed big branches from trees cut down like there had been a storm with lightning strikes. There must have been at least five lots of branches in the creek that were freshly cut from the mother tree. However, there hadn't been a storm that afternoon and we were going back down the same creek we had come up.

I asked, "Clint, can you see those eyes up there about 50 m ahead?" He replied, "Yes, Dad. I saw them a couple of minutes ago but I didn't want to say anything." The spirit figure was about 3 m tall, with one red eye and one blue eye. Each of the eyes was nearly 30 cm across. We didn't talk much after that. We were just glad to get out of the jungle and back to our camp. I haven't been back. Something there was telling me not to go back.

From what I've been told by local Aboriginal people, I believe the Tchuken Bora Ground is reasonably close to a sacred site. This could explain some vexatious spirits guarding the site. Some locals have told me they won't go near that place because of a big hairy man, otherwise known as a Yowie. If we were close to that site, that would explain the red and blue eyes that we encountered and the busted limbs off the trees in the creek that weren't there when we traversed it in the morning.

The last man from that area to be afforded a traditional burial was someone with the initials FD. He was carried in a coffin in the rain to his final resting place under a tree. We never did find the Tchuken Bora Ground, but we did find the Chunga Bora Ground and a Bora Ground up in the Goldsborough Valley about 40 kilometres from Cairns.

The name "Bora" has different meanings and connotations for different tribal groups in Australia. Some say the word Bora was originally from South East Australia. It has been used and is still being used throughout Eastern Australia to describe an initiation site or ceremony.

In some parts of Australia, Bora rings are mandala-like formations that comprise circles of foot- hardened earth surrounded by raised embankments. They were generally constructed in pairs with the biggest circle about 22m in diameter and a smaller one of about 14m. The rings are joined by a sacred walkway. Bora rings, in the form of circles of individually placed stones, have been found in the Werrikimbe National Park in the North of NSW.

CHAPTER 3

THE DROWNING CHINESE GIRL

Kurramine Beach is approximately 40 km south of Innisfail in North Queensland. It's a quiet little township primarily regarded as a fishing village. The Great Barrier Reef is only about 3 to 400m from the shoreline. July is when the tide reaches its lowest point during the year. This is the time of year that the greatest amount of reef is exposed as the tide goes out much more than any other time.

It is possible to walk from the shoreline as the tide recedes, spend some time exploring the exposed reef, and walk back to shore. Many people have done it, me included, but the trick is to take note when the tide is due to turn back and start walking to shore straight away. Otherwise, the incoming tide can surprise you and rise at a speed much faster than what is anticipated. Anyone who can't swim might drown in the rapidly rising water.

The day was 25 January 1993. I'd taken my three children and a neighbour's girl for a walk along the beach. We sat down on an old wooden bridge in the mangroves and the children searched for baby crabs and anything else that looked like it was moving. It was one of their favourite places, exactly why I don't know. However, they enjoyed it and that's all that really mattered with a little running creek and nature in the palm of your hand.

We'd been at the bridge for about 20 minutes, when I observed a group of three people wading in the water with some waving their hands. I thought they were saying hello to us and didn't take much more notice until I thought I could hear a voice calling for help. The group was still waving but it was difficult to make out if they were in distress because they were in water that was only chest-height.

I diverted my attention for a while, thinking I must be hearing voices. However, I heard the distant sound of voices more distinctly, this time again crying, "Help." I had a really difficult decision to make. Our youngest child, Ryan, was only a little over three years old and at that point hadn't learned to swim. Somehow, I had to find a way to convince him to go back with the other children to their mum who was about a kilometre away. My eldest son and the neighbour's girl were about 10 years of age. I gave them the task of taking Ryan back home to his mum. He didn't want to go and they had to physically drag him since he was calling out that he wanted to go in with Dad. My worst nightmare was Ryan breaking free and following me into the water. As I entered the water, I heard the sounds of Ryan screaming out, "Dad! Dad!"

The trio I was going out to help was approximately 300m from the shoreline. I started to swim towards them. While I was swimming, somebody from a caravan park saw the dilemma, launched his boat, and arrived where the three people were calling out for help. I arrived at precisely the same time. The girl was still thrashing about. I attended to her first and got her up over the edge of the boat and into the boat. The other two were floating and weren't moving at all.

I lifted the smallest male up over the edge of the boat and into the boat. I repeated doing this with the other much larger male who was nearly twice the size of the first man. I got into the boat and tried mouth-to-mouth resuscitation on the male that looked like he had the most life in him, if there was any at all. I pushed and was ready to resuscitate, when a large amount of water gushed out of his mouth. I tried the process again and more water gushed out. I tried repeatedly to breathe a spark of life into the man but it was to no avail. His skin was deathly cold an had no pulse. I tried so much that I got physically sick myself and vomited on the floor of the boat. At the same time, my false teeth fell out of my mouth and landed on the bottom of the boat. The skipper of the boat did no try to resuscitate the second male while I was trying to save the larger of the two.

When we had reached the boat ramp, a crowd of onlookers had appeared curious to find out if any of the three people survived. The Chinese girl was as large as life but for the other two lives, they had departed. I left the crowd and went home to check if my youngest child had made it home safely. I was very relieved that he had. It would have been a very high price to pay: to lose my youngest child to save another human being.

I got a call from the local police the next day, wondering if I'd lost my false teeth. The ambulance guys apparently saw them in the bottom of the boat and thought they belonged to one of the deceased. He, therefore, put them in the ambulance with the deceased. Upon arrival at the mortuary, they noticed that the deceased all had full sets of teeth and they had a spare set. Hence, the phone call from the police officer.

Apparently, what had happened was that the three people involved in this tragedy had come from James Cook University in Townsville to walk out to the reef at low tide in July. What became their undoing was that none of them could swim. They spent too much time observing the reef. They didn't notice that the tide had turned and was rising for quite some time before they started their fateful journey back to the shore. As the tide crept up on them, they began to panic. That was when I saw them waving their hands and crying for help. When I last looked, as I swam out to them, I was only about 100m from the trio and, in that short time, two drowned.

The girl that I helped save wrote to me on a beautiful handmade Chinese panda card six months later, thanking me for saving her life. At that time, she was going to university in America but, over time, we've lost contact. The police officer that attended the scene nominated me for a bravery award and I was awarded one from the Governor General under the patronage of her Majesty the Queen.

Kurramine Beach was the place where the children experienced Mother Nature in all her finery. Now as an adult, my youngest child, Ryan, has returned to Kurramine with his employment. When he's not raising a sweat as a chef in the kitchen at a local resort, he spends many leisure hours fishing.

Apart from camping in exotic places and swimming in pristine waters in the jungle, the children all were involved in sports like rugby league, soccer, and cricket. Every second weekend we travelled to another town in North Queensland where the children participated in their chosen sport. We travelled many miles going to these activities. The greatest lesson that I learned was from our eldest, Clinton.

He was extremely gifted in any sport he played but he didn't think whatever he gave was good enough. There were times he was the best player on the field by far and he still didn't think he was good enough. I didn't know at the time but Clinton's lesson would ultimately be a lesson for me to learn, because at a spiritual level I didn't think I was good enough in Christ's eyes.

I would reflect, "Before you take the speck out of your brother's eyes, take the plank out of your own."(cf Matthew 3)

Christ quoted from Psalm 82 to prove his Messianic credentials. His citation of Psalm 82:6 must be explored with the larger context of John's Gospel, "I say you are gods; you are all sons of the Most High." When Jesus spoke of the miracles he performed he said, "I tell you whoever believes in me, those works which I have done he will also do – nay, more than that." (John 4:36-38)

As well as the first two Commandments, these two pieces of scripture have stayed forever etched in my soul. When I first read them, I originally thought it would be blasphemy to do what Christ was advocating in the Scriptures. I thought there must have been an error in the translation. Who was I to go close to the amazing miracles that Christ had performed? Yet here it was in black and white telling me I could walk this road.

It all started with just one step on my journey to awaken the Christ Consciousness within. This awakening would take place over time. This process continues for me to this day, even as I write this book. There is rejoicing in the heavens when a seeker awakens his and her Christ consciousness. The archangels are filled with joy when they see us returning to our divine nature. Edgar Cayce explained the awakening process by saying, "Jesus was like each one of us and, ultimately, each one of us is destined to be like him." The Gnostics have a beautiful quote that says, "If you know the spirit, you become the spirit." My awakening ran almost parallel to my entry into the secret, sacred world of the Australian Aborigine. It began at Upper Murray near Tully when I first saw the fifteen Aboriginal figures from the astral world.

From Kurramine Beach, we moved back to the town of Innisfail and rented a house on Flying Fish Point Road. For the children, this was probably one of their happiest times of their childhood with wide-open spaces between the sugarcane crops, hills to climb, swimming holes and even a crocodile farm right next door. We still went camping on a regular basis and, quite often when it rained, I made a fire under a shelter and cooked damper. They just loved their damper with butter and syrup.

It was during this period that I really started to seek some answers which had perplexed me for most of my lifetime. The indigenous component really had me mystified. I wrote a letter to a band called Yothu Yindi from a place called Nhulunbuy in the Northern Territory. They were a red-hot Aboriginal band back then and in the ensuing years, they would carve themselves a name as the hottest Aboriginal band that ever was. The disappointment for me was that I had written to the lead singer who never answered my correspondence. This was a blessing because the next person I wrote to was David Mowaljarlai in Derby, Western Australia.

David returned my letter and on top of that, made a phone call to me at my workplace. It is probably the most important phone call that I've ever received. He acknowledged my request and reiterated that "The Wandjina have come to you." While I understood what he was saying was important, I really didn't understand what he meant. It would be nearly twenty years before I understood the real meaning of what he was talking about.

It wasn't until I studied the work of Daskalos' Researchers of Truth that I was able to understand that the Wandjinas are archangels. It is believed there are twelve Archangelic Orders: Thrones, Authorities, Dominions, Principalities, Overlords, Seraphims, and Cherubims among others. The Wandjinas don't have a mouth because their power is so great that they don't need to speak. As a result, their communication occurs at an entirely different level. The archangels are spirit beings who have never been born and will never die. They are eternal.

Through spiritual discipline, we can come in conscious communication with these great intelligences. They welcome us and are ready to reveal their great wisdom to us when we have attuned to their frequency. Few have come close enough to these Orders to attune to them, but I can definitely vouch for the Wandjinas being living, breathing spirit beings. This is because I've seen and communicated with them in broad daylight. Once again, I didn't tell a soul since most indigenous people that I knew, had never heard of a Wandjina. In addition, the chances of a non-indigenous person having seen one must be completely off this planet.

At around the same time, I applied for membership to the Rosicrucian Society. I was accepted and started diligent study. I even had my own little room for a temple. I studied for eighteen months and got bold enough to start asking questions. My first question was if there was anyone in the Rosicrucian Society that understood the shaman aspect of Australian Aboriginal culture. They were unable to answer my question, since they didn't have anybody in their organisation that had studied this aspect of the mysteries.

While they weren't able to shed any light on this aspect of Aboriginal culture, I benefited greatly from learning their meditation techniques. I practiced every time I had some quiet time to myself. I was pleased because I was gettingbeneficial results on my first attempt. Within months, I was able to have out-of-body experiences at regular intervals and I was finally able to access the Cosmic Consciousness with ease.

In one of these experiences, I travelled vast distances to a tropical island. Here, I was given seven crosses, each representing a spiritual gift from the seven Masters on the island. The detail was so concise that I can recall the crosses being what we call today the Budded Cross. I can remember encountering a man on the island who was very angry with me. With just the power of my mind, I was able to draw his anger out and leave him a happy soul once again. Through these out-of-body experiences, I was able to learn much about the power of the mind. I also found myself able to transfer the experiences from the astral realm into real life experiences in the third dimension on Mother Earth. On numerous occasions, I was able to look into an angry person's eyes and draw out the anger without a word and just with my mind. This is what I'd been taught on the island with the seven Masters.

The latest Russian scientific research, directly or indirectly, explains phenomena such as clairvoyance, intuition, spontaneous and remote access healing, and affirmation techniques. Esoteric and spiritual teachers have long known that our body is programmable by language, words and thought. This has now been scientifically proven and explained thanks to Russian scientists.

I was entering into another world while leaving my footprints in the dust on Mother Earth. My meditations kept going to deeper levels. As soon as I had my mind still enough, Beta waves would fill my brain with a frequency of 13-40 cycles per second Hz. My research informed me the next stage was a dominance of Alpha waves with a frequency of 8-12 Hz. When I went lower to Theta waves 4-7 Hz, it was as though this world didn't exist. At 0.5-3 Hz, I was reaching a state of consciousness call my "Higher Self."

The periods of "oneness" came more frequently and lasted longer. During one of these periods, I tasted *Amrita*, which is known as the nectar of the gods. It is secreted from the throat chakra when activated and has a taste that I could only describe as coming from another world. I found my voice reflecting the condition of my mind and I marveled at its power. At this level, I believe that my highest expression became manifest and my thoughts became action.

I struggle to verbalise this other world I was becoming to know. One way of doing this is to share a story from that amazing Indian warrior called Crazy Horse. When Crazy Horse went into vision, he said that the real world, the one he sees in vision in the fourth dimension, was the real world and that everything else we see on planet Earth is like a shadow of that one. He was on his horse in that world, and the horse, himself, and the trees, grass, and stones – everything was made of spirit and nothing was hard and everything seemed to float. This is a near identical account of how Daskalos describes the fourth dimension and beyond.

Many other aspects of my being began to surface. I started horse riding again after an absence of twenty-two years. I also started writing poetry early in the morning nearly every morning. I was awake between 4-4:30 AM. and made my way to a shed that was adjacent to the house where I wrote on a very special table. I made this table in Kurramine Beach out of Johnston River hardwood, which is now an extremely rare timber in North Queensland. The reason I made it by hand was so that I could follow in the steps that Jesus had laid before us all. I wanted to feel as he felt when he was a carpenter. I wanted to feel every drop of sweat and every movement of his hand. I wanted to walk just for a little bit in his footsteps.

On this table, I wrote over 200 poems over an eighteen-month period. I won some competitions with some of them and even had a couple published. I was then invited to a big poetry festival in the United States. Willie Nelson and other celebrities were performing at the same event. I was very tempted to go but there was a question of money and we had to get ourselves there and back home again. I've included some poems from that period in this book. I am very passionate about those poems.

My love of horses is only equaled by my love of life. My dreams would come true every second Sunday at a place called Garradunga. I would ride a chestnut mare at a friend's place. She was an ex- racehorse and every time I rode her, inevitably, she would try to buck me off. I've ridden some pretty wild horses in my life and she wasn't one of them. Every time I rode her around 500 m from the house, she would inevitably start to buck. I had become quite an accomplished rider by then. She never managed to buck hard enough to throw me off onto the ground. Once that ritual was over, we would go off on the byways and backways of Garradunga. Sometimes, we would venture into some of the most pristine rainforest wilderness in the world.

We travelled mile after mile and I would become at one with everything around me. I would take my poetry-writing book and pen and, quite often, I would write some of my best poems from these exotic locations. On one particular ride out, I saw two rainforest dingoes (wild dogs): one was jet black and the other an orange colour. What was peculiar about these dingoes was that they were quite short. They were only half the size of our ordinary dingo. They are quite rare and now quite possibly extinct. Rainforest Aborigines were also short in stature. We are told that living in a rainforest environment, it was beneficial to be closer to the ground when traversing through the forest. As a result, over time, this group of Aborigines were more of a pygmy size.

The chestnut mare belonged to special friends of ours, Doug and Elrae, from Diggers Creek. I quite would often give Doug a hand with his cattle in return for riding the chestnut mare. We would brand the young calves, cut a piece out of the ear with earmarking pliers to identify them, and inoculate them with a serum to stop them from catching various diseases. I would often stay and have lunch with Doug and Elrae.

Apart from the fact that I was enjoying horse riding again, something else was going on. My consciousness was being raised to levels that I had not experienced before. Every time I rode, I was having a similar experience. One particular morning on my way out to a remote rainforest, I had a vision. This was my third one by now, so I was fully aware what was happening. Apart from a regular pretend-bucking interlude when I first rode her out, this mare was also apt to shy and go sideways at a great pace when something spooked her.

So vision or no vision, I needed to have my wits about me the whole time I rode her. I was in the middle of this vision while at the same time fully conscious of who I was, where I was, and what I was doing. In the vision, I was on top of a cleared area on the side of a mountain and I was in a radio studio doing a talkback radio show. My audience thousands of people, and they were all listening in their houses at the bottom of the ocean. They didn't have radios. They could hear what I was broadcasting just by attuning themselves to me. It was similar to the way I had described attuning oneself to the Wandjina archangels or other archangels. In the Researchers of Truth, they describe water as a metaphor for etheric vitality also called our *daily bread*. These people existed in a sea of etheric vitality that was sustaining them as they listened, or absorbing the radio program I was broadcasting. They exist in the astral realm or the fourth dimension in the same world that Crazy Horse described a little earlier.

Once again, I didn't tell a soul. I went on my way up into the beautiful pristine rainforest, put my leg strap on the front two legs of my horse so she wouldn't run away, and then wrote poetry. I didn't try to interpret the vision because, since it was my third vision, I'd found these things unfold in time. I'd had quite a number of out-of-body experiences as well and it was the same with them: in time, all will be revealed.

The years we lived on Flying Fish Point Road were a very special time for my family. I had built the kids a go-cart out of spare material from around the farm. It was at this time that the movie *Cool Runnings* was popular. The only difference was that my three boys encountered the red dirt of a cane farm as opposed to the ice as portrayed in the movie. There were many hills on this cane farm and some of them had a steep angle of descent. However, this was just the adrenaline fix that the boys were looking for. Just like the movie, they came down the hills at a near death-defying pace. They wore helmets which was all the body protection that they had. Sometimes, they rolled the go-cart off the road and into the cane paddock. There were no major injuries, only some skin off and a bit of bleeding. The strangest part of it all was that the youngest son was the fastest. I had a stopwatch which I used to time them. He always recorded the fastest. He had absolutely no fear at all and, of course, this frustrated the two older boys.

Everywhere we went the two dogs came too. The oldest one was part Alsatian and part Kelpie. The other one was an Australian blue cattle dog. At nighttime, we used to play hidey-go-seek and the part-Alsatian part-Kelpie would set out to find the three boys after she was let off the chain. We would tie her up first and count to 20 while the kids hid, then we'd let her off and she would sniff and follow their tracks. She was so good I could call out one of the boy's name and she would track him down first.

This was after the boys ran around over the top of each other's tracks half a dozen times. She could still pick out that one boy's individual track and find him. Ryan, the youngest, would get terribly upset if she found him first and he would get cranky with the dog. Many a night, we played this same game and the dog inevitably found where they were hiding.

It was also around the time on television when they had shows on like *The Gladiators*. The contestants did all kinds of crazy things testing the contestant's physical endurance. The children were quite hooked on this show, so I built some of the same sorts of things that were on the television program in our backyard. It was a bit like an obstacle course that they have in the Army to condition the troops. I'd use the stopwatch to time their performance and they just loved it. They grew up with a love of the outdoors and if they were watching a video game and using foul language, I would just turn the TV off and say "Outside!"

My meditations continued and deepened. The images were becoming clearer and much more distinct. In one session, I saw a Buddha with a strange conical type headdress. I did some research to see if such a Buddha existed and, sure enough, he does. Well kind of, because he is the Buddha that is yet to come. He has not manifested himself on the earth plane yet. He's called the Maitreya Buddha.

A few months later, I saw another Buddha. This time he was made up of thousands and thousands of diamonds all glowing brightly. As I watched, the diamonds turned into pure light. It was light but it was a different kind of light that was bright yet at the same time soft. I could nearly reach out and touch it.

Through research, I was able to find that according to Buddhist tradition, Maitreya is a Bodhisattva who will appear on earth in the future, achieve complete enlightenment, and teach the pure dharma. Maitreya will be a successor to the present Buddha, Gautama Buddha. Maitreya currently resides in the Tusita heaven (Pali: Tusita), which is said to be reachable through meditation. Gautama Buddha also lived there before he was born into the world. All Bohisvattas live in Tusita heaven before they descend to the human realm to become Buddhas.

Daskalos of the Researchers of Truth shared a great insight with the world when he revealed that Buddha, in fact, had predicted Christ's coming 500 years before the event. Buddha had said, "I have shown you a way but He is going to complete this way. He Himself will be the Way, the Truth and the Life."

Prior to these visions in my meditations, I had had very little to do with the Buddhist tradition apart from attending a day here in Cairns when they brought the relics of the Buddha and other Buddhist Masters. The Maitreya Heart Shrine Relic Tour of 2012 was a unique and precious collection of more than 1000 sacred relics that would be permanently displayed in the Heart Shrine of the completed Maitreya Buddha statue in Kushinagar. It was the wish of the Spiritual Director of the Maitreya Project that the collection should travel throughout the world to bring the blessings of the relics and the message of the loving kindness to people everywhere. I visited these amazing relics at the Khacho Yulo Ling Buddhist Centre in Cairns.

Most of the relics, including those found among the cremation ashes of Buddhist Masters, resemble beautiful pearls like crystals. Buddhas believe these relics are produced because of the Masters' spiritual qualities of compassion and wisdom. Since we can all develop these qualities, the relics are a reminder of our own essential nature of purity and potential to manifest that.

I experienced some of these blessings as one of the women, accompanying the relics, asked me to sit for a blessing. She ran her hands over my head and said, "You have been blessed." I could feel this beautiful energy run from my head right to the soles my feet. I felt so uplifted that my feet barely touched the ground on the way to our car.

It is said that after Buddha's death, he was cremated and the ashes were divided among his disciples. His ashes were originally to go to the Sakya clan, to which Buddha belonged. However, seven royal families demanded the body relics and, to avoid fighting, a monk divided the relics into 10 portions. It is said that all of the Buddhas' relics will one day gather at the Bodhi tree where he attained enlightenment and will then form his body, sitting cross-legged and performing the twin miracle.

As this book unfolds and yields its inner secrets, it will have crossed a number of spiritual traditions, starting with the Aboriginal Dreamtime, the longest continuous religion in the world. It will have engaged Christianity, Buddhism, the teachings of Daskalos, the Researchers of Truth, the teachings of Edgar Cayce, the world of the Native American Indians, and the teachings of the Gnostics.

Beyond spirituality and religion, I'll also peek down the rabbit hole into the world of quantum physics. In the world of Professor Stephen Hawking, he claimed (01/05/2016) that black holes are other gateways to mysterious alternative dimensions. *The Lion, the Witch and the Wardrobe* by C. S. Lewis, was the gateway to a parallel universe locked away at the back of the cupboard that the siblings Peter, Susan, Edmund, and Lucy Pevensie discovered.

Alice in Wonderland, a novel written by the English mathematician Charles Lutwidge Dodgson, under the pseudonym Lewis Carroll, wanted to visit the alternative reality of Wonderland as she squeezed herself down a rabbit hole. However, if you're like Stephen Hawking, the most efficient way of visiting another dimension is to throw yourself bravely into the gaping maw of a black hole.

During a recent speech at Harvard University, the British physicist claimed black holes "are backdoors and aren't the eternal presence they were once thought." According to Professor Hawking, things get out of a black hole, both from the outside and possibly through another universe. He said, "If you feel you're in a black hole, don't give up. There's a way out." Professor Hawking is on a mission to make us rethink our negative preconceptions of black holes.

Earlier this year, he said we could power the whole of human society, if it if we could only somehow harness the energy of the amount and and size of a black hole. However, with great power comes great risk. If we fail to control the black hole, it could sink into the middle of Earth and begin feasting on human beings, our home planet and, eventually, the entire solar system. He said, "A mountain-size black hole would give off x-rays and gamma rays at a rate of about 10 million MW, enough to power the world's electricity supply."

This thinking is not that far removed from what Daskalos and the Researchers of Truth have spoken of for many decades. Daskalos spoke of the third dimension, Earth, and of two other worlds parallel to our world. More to the point, he taught how we can reach these other worlds. Some Aboriginal people of Australia know of these worlds and can access them quite easily. Western civilisation calls these worlds The Dreamtime. It is true that you can visit these worlds in your dreams, but it is a misnomer to call all these worlds Dreamtime as there are other worlds beyond.

You can access the dreamtime world while awake or through meditation.

It is to one of these worlds we go when we die. Each of us has a distinct rate of vibration. The Sufis call it our "tome" and according to our specific tome when we pass over, we go to a plane with a corresponding rate of vibration in the astral realm. Archangels accompany us to our new environment and although we are able to go down from the plane in which we are assigned to a lower one, we cannot go up to a higher plan. This is because the light would be too bright for that soul at this point of his or her journey.

The earliest contact I can recall with the indigenous world at a deeply spiritual level was during an out-of-body experience I had in January 2013. My mind travelled back in time to a place in North East Arnhem land where I met my "Yolngu" mother. She was under a tree smoking a Macaasan pipe. She spoke in Yolngu, her native tongue, and I understood what she was saying. She said, "You've had your initiations and you have been through law, you're doing great. Don't doubt yourself."

The Yolgnu had traded with the Macaasans 600 years before Captain Cook landed in Australia. At that time, there were 500 Aboriginal nations within the borders of Australia. It's like saying there were 500 countries such as Austria, Belgium, Sweden, etc. There were 500 different languages spoken along with subdialects of each language. The Yolgnu nation was and still is one of the largest Aboriginal groups in Australia and for most, English is still a second language.

I don't differentiate between what is called "real" and an out-of-body experience, since I perceive each one to be just as real as the other. The experience of a lifetime occurred when I walked down a sacred ceremonial trail of an ancient Bora Ground at Nine Mile at the tender age of eight years. Nine Mile was a property my dad owned inland from Rockhampton in Central Queensland and not far from a little township called Comet. My next major contact with the Aboriginal world was the time I visited the Stockman's Hall of Fame. I saw the dots on the dot painting spinning round at a high speed until they all converged into lines. There was also a time when I saw a painting in Kuranda from Utopia in Central Australia and I was able to view it in 3-D.

There was also the vision I saw of Aboriginal people in the spirit world when I visited Upper Murray Falls near Tully. I was 25 years at the time but I still didn't understand what this was all going to mean to me. As usual, I didn't tell a soul.

Following that experience, there was a group of Aboriginal people on the Esplanade in Cairns and since I had another out-of-body experience, the leader of the group motioned for me to follow them. I felt Christ was calling me but he kept showing up as indigenous people and that just left me confused. Was it possible for Christ to use Aboriginal people to show me a different way to live life that was quite different from the Western way of life I was used to? Was I meant to look into their world? And of what possible use would that be?

After 15 years of marriage, my wife and I split. Our youngest son, Ryan, expressed a desire to be with me. His mum was okay with that and he moved in with me in a caravan park on the North Johnston River in Innisfail. He kept going to his normal school and every second weekend I would pick up Clinton and Sean and take them to their various sporting events that they were involved in. We would spend many of the spare hours in the numerous swimming holes around North Queensland. In summer and winter, we dedicated more time to travelling, exploring, and camping.

I also tried to educate the three boys into knowing what and when "bush tucker" was available as we travelled around. We tried wild guava, white apple, Burdekin plum, Davidson's plum, pipi's, lillypillies, mud crab, along with the more traditional roast beef and veggies cooked in the camp oven using the slow coals of a fire. There was always plenty of damper (damper is a mixture of flour and water, sometimes with a little butter and honey) cooked in a camp oven and most trips we had a good supply of steak that we cooked on the dying embers of the fire. They grew up thinking this was a normal way of life but little did they know very few children had the same opportunities to experience this big wide land as they did.

One bush tucker experiment that didn't go so well was freshwater mussels out of the river. We harvested them okay and we had plenty. We got the usual fire going, waited until it died down to coals and then placed the food on top. Sit back and wait is the usual method and that's what we did. I'm not sure if we overstated exactly how good these were going to be or we cooked them the wrong way, but whatever way you look at it, they turned out as tough as boots. I kid you not; this was the worst bush tucker we had ever tasted.

One of our favourite camping spots was on Henrietta Creek in the Wooroornooran National Park. This is a world-heritage-listed pristine rainforest. There's probably no rainforest in the world that is much better than this. In fact, tourists from all over the world come and marvel at its beauty, while the locals seem a little oblivious to it all.

I recently learned that an enterprising Australian company called "Green and Clean Air" is bottling air from places like this and selling it as an aerosol can to cities in other parts of the world that have polluted their air. It is selling for $18 a can, complete with mouthpiece, just to breathe in unpolluted air for a short while. Each can contains 130 to 140 puffs. It's a business bound for really big things in a market that sees bad quality air killing 1.6 million Chinese annually. The consumers who buy this product, generally like to inhale it upon waking first thing in the morning. The good thing is, in Australia, most of our country has non-polluted air.

While on these camping trips, we came across someone well known from this area, but now deceased: FD. There was another name that was regularly mentioned as well: Joe Brooks. His Aboriginal name was Matcho. However, who he was and what he did remained an enigma for 20 years, until I started to write this book. I asked for information from some of the descendants of his family name but the storyline had grown a little thin considering that it began nearly 100 years ago.

Joe, as he was known, was more than likely born under a tree in the bush. However, the exact year is unknown. His life was destined to intertwine with a Swedish chiropractor called Ernst Kjellberg who, with his wife Louise, made their way to Mila Milla in North Queensland in 1920. He was helped by local Aborigines, some of whom would become life-long employees, to clear a 160-acre selection outside Milla Milla. This is where he opened up his extensive Beachview Clinic in 1920. By the 1930s, large numbers of patients were receiving Kjellberg's manipulative therapy, often with remarkable results.

The part Joe Brooks played in these results is open to debate. I've spoken to distant relatives and with the kind help from David at the Eacham Historical Society, I've been able to piece together parts of Joe Brook's life. In whispered tones, I found out that Joe Brooks was a healer and some even say, a "Magic

Man" or "Clever Man." It's not impossible to fathom that Joe was applying his trade at the Beachview Clinic.

At its peak, Beachview was home to up to 500 clients and employees. Pictures of Beachview available from the Eacham Historical Society give a vivid account of the Kjellberg dynasty. Many patients lived on site, sometimes accompanied by family members who helped with general tasks in lieu of payment. A number of other buildings, including a gymnasium, were constructed while many staff, patients and their families were accommodated. Imagine the price of an airline ticket from Austria or Germany in the 1920s. The first commercial airplane flight with paying passengers only commenced in 1914. Therefore, something pretty amazing must've been happening at Beachview by the 1930s for hundreds of clients to reside there at one time.

Beachview closed in 1950 but by then a clinic was operating in Townsville and also in Cairns. Ernest Kjellberg died in 1968 and was buried with his wife in the Belgian Garden Cemetery. Notably, one of his most loyal Aboriginal employees, Joe Brooks, was also buried on the same site. In a day when blacks and whites were segregated in some parts of Australia, it shows the reverence that Ernst must've held for his beloved friend, Joe Brooks.

These were the days when transport was changing from wooden carts drawn by horses to the Model T Ford that revolutionised the way people lived. It was also a time of racism in Australia that it would like to erase from her blackboard of history. Less than 100 years ago, the Coniston massacre occurred, killing 30 Aboriginal people in the Northern Territory. Blacks and whites were separated at the movies and quite often at swimming pools. In fact, blacks and whites were rarely seen together.

The Aboriginal Protection Board was meant to ease the tensions and to fix Aboriginal problems. What they did was take children away from their parents and place them in white training institutions call "missions." The belief was that if they took the brown-coloured children away, the black children and the full bloods would breed out, since their parents were destined to die out in this generation. In fact, the Western Australian Premier Forest has quite openly stated this. This generation is now known as the Stolen Generation and many have struggled with depression.

Aboriginal people of that era often worked for 16 hours a day and only received a fraction of what a white man would have received. In fact, right from the time of Federation, the Constitution stated that Aboriginal natives would not be counted as people. Instead, they were still regarded as flora and fauna. This blight on Australia's history would remain until a 1967 referendum declared Aboriginal people to be members of the human race. Each state in the Commonwealth had power over Aboriginal affairs. An example of this is when in 1909, New South Wales introduced the New South Wales Aborigines Act following crises in public schools. Exclusion of Aboriginal children from public schools resulted in a request by the European community to set up Aboriginal schools. By 1920, there were 35 schools in New South Wales.

The Aboriginal population in Australia in 1920 was estimated to be 60,000. It was widely believed they were a "dying race." It wasn't until 1965 that the last nomadic Aborigines that were living entirely off the land were brought into "civilisation." The Pintubi people were relocated to Papunya and Yendumu.

The Aborigines who left their ancestral lands or who were forcibly removed were herded onto missions. The missions were essentially prison camps. Indigenous people were denied their land rights and voting rights. They couldn't leave or return without permission, couldn't possess alcohol and had limited access to the justice system. Authorities had the power to remove children, forbid marriages, censor mail, and compel them to work for low wages, withhold wages, control bank accounts and seize property.

These were also the days of what has come to be known as "The Massacres." A Cairns author recently released a book on the subject. The number of massacres that took place is frightening. At Old Mapoon, there were roughly 300 residents in the early 1900s. Since they were competing for land with the new pastoralists, the pastoralists took matters into their own hands. Out of 300 people, only 50 survived. I've heard a similar story echoed from the top of the Northern Territory and Queensland right across to WA and Victoria.

This was Australia's version of apartheid, a black history of which only a few Australians are aware of today. Some Queenslanders have a vague memory of the time in 1963 when an armed detachment of Queensland police arrived at the Aboriginal community of Mapoon. They had orders to forcibly remove 23 Aboriginal residents and to commence demolition of the vacated shanties on the reserve. A shameful history that occurred during my lifetime wasn't to end there. Herded into boats like cattle, Aborigines were taken to their new home nearly at the top of Australia to a place called New Mapoon.

It may have been new but it certainly wasn't their ancestral lands. Over time slowly but surely they all came back to what was home and rebuilt using the very most basic of building items like the old sheets of corrugated iron. The rest of the materials came from the bush. I know personally one of the women that walked that walk, hundreds of kilometres on foot. Why would a government burn a township to the ground - this country's very first inhabitants?

The truth lay in the fact that in the 1950s, a discovery of bauxite was unearthed in Western Cape. It was the biggest deposit in the world. Large areas of land were granted as mining leases to Comalco and Alcan. Given this background, it is even more amazing that Joe Brooks was interred with his employer and wife in a Townsville cemetery. Their friendship and a bind that was almost blood is one of the most remarkable stories I've encountered since I first walked that ancient Bora Ground Trail over 50 years ago.

CHAPTER 4

THE RAINBOW SERPENT

My ultimate goal when I set out on my spiritual path was Self Realization. That was my Mount Everest, my Nirvana and my everything. I always thought of it as something I had to conquer and that it would take most of my life to achieve it. Like many things in life, the reality is quite often different from the illusion that we have created over time.

The same is true with Self Realization. One day while driving the car in April 2016, it occurred to me that "I am a perfect soul,". That's exactly who I am: a perfectly incorruptible spirit Soul, no big fanfare, no big clanging of drums, just this complete realisation. I had been building this awareness slowly over the years, brick by brick. From a distance, when I turned around and surveyed my work, those bricks had now formed a wall.

In a way my book has been completed. I could stop writing right now but there is still so much more to share. Along the way, I found:

God is bigger than my past
Bigger than my depression
Bigger than my pain
Bigger than my self-depreciation
Bigger than my anger

Bigger than my doubt
Bigger than my fear
Bigger than my shame
And bigger than my anxiety

The Lord I had come to know was not to be feared. I found a friend and the one place I felt closest to him more than any other over the years is a little creek near Cairns called Freshwater Creek. Nestled away on its creek bank, is a piece of heaven called Goomboora Park. It's about 5 acres snuggled in the rainforest. I have been visiting this little creek since 1999. This is my *church*, the water is holy and if I'm lucky and there's not too many people around, my level of vibration increases immensely. Here I can come in conscious contact with the archangels, but only if I get completely still within my mind.

I've been there twice today and on a recent visit I reminded myself that this creek is home to the Rainbow Serpent. The water python is also known as the Rainbow Serpent. Its scales are an iridescent dark grey colour that reflects the colours of a rainbow when taken out of the water. I've seen this for myself when a young lad about 12 years of age caught one. There were distinct lines of colour like the rainbow running parallel down its back.

Some of the youth used to play with these snakes and throw them about. I thought they must have frightened them all off with their rough treatment since I hadn't seen one in eighteen months. Imagine my joy as I went into the water. I looked and looked again. It looks like a snake. Praise the Lord; it's a water python! It was coming towards me (and I'm aware they can bite), so I swam over the top of it to where I wanted to go. Shout it from the mountaintops. Let it be known the Rainbow Serpent is back in Freshwater Creek. Some people swim with whales, some swim with the dolphins, but Greg Reid swims with the Rainbow Serpent.

Water pythons inhabit freshwater swamps, lagoons, creeks, and rivers across the tropical North of Australia. Water pythons have also been found in the Torres Straits and Papua New Guinea. They are very fond of water and in the wild frequently use water as an escape route. Water pythons feed on rats, bandicoots, wallabies, water birds (and their eggs) and have been seen feeding on small freshwater crocodiles. Their prey is usually ambushed when it comes to drink. A juvenile water python's diet consists of frogs, fish and lizards. Water pythons generally grow to a size of around 2 m. Breeding tends to commence with a flurry of mating activity in February and March with eggs being laid some weeks later. The female water python usually lays between 11 and 19 eggs.

The National Indigenous Times newspaper told a story of Malaluba Gumana and a painting she did called "Dhatam" which is the story of Wititj of storm and monsoon in her ancestral past. It has particular reference to the mating of the Rainbow Serpent during the beginning of the wet season. That coincides with an earlier comment that we now recognise the water python mates in the February and March period, which is the beginning of the wet season in the North.

The Rainbow Serpent is commonly referred as a mythical being in the creation of this world. The word mythical doesn't sit well with me. It is the same way I imagine people would be upset if we were to refer to Jesus as being mythical. However, in this book, I tried my best to relate its holy story with reverence. It is, in fact, the oldest religious belief system in the world which continues to this day. For different tribal groups, there is a variation in the telling of the creation story.

As I've travelled this road, I have intensively studied the work of the Researchers of Truth. From their perspective, I was able to understand the creation story Ngarinyin of the Kimberley as handed down by Mabel King, David Mowaljarlai, and others.

According to Mowanjum, artist Mabel King during the Lai Lai (the creation time), Wallungunder the big boss Wandjina came from the Milky Way to create the earth and all the people. Wallungunder was the son of Idjair (the emu). The first people were the Gyorn Gyorn, whichsome white people call the Bradshaw figures who were named after the first white person to see them in 1891. The Gyorn Gyorn had no laws or kinship and wandered around lost.

Wallungunder saw he could do well with these people and brought many other Wandjinas with the power of the Dreamtime snake to help him bring laws and kinship to the Gyorn Gyorn people. The Dreamtime Snake represents Mother Earth and it is called Ungud. Each of the artists has his own ungud birthplace or dreaming place.

Edgar Cayce stated, "The first souls descended from heaven to the Earth plane and began incarnating as humans. This first wave of souls to incarnate was known in the Bible as the 'sons of men' and they become entrapped in the Earth plane accidentally, through their misuse of free will."

He said, "The second wave of incarnations (known in the Bible as 'the sons of God') consisted of those souls led by the Christ Soul who become voluntarily entrapped in order to assist the first wave of trapped souls. This was accomplished by steering the process of physical evolution in a way that created more appropriate physical forms for these souls." He added, "The Christ Soul did not physically incarnate until the human physical form had been created, at which time the Genesis accounts of

Adam and Eve begin." Cayce refers to the word "Adam" as an entire group of souls which accompanied the Christ Soul into the incarnating into the Earth plane.

The Researchers of Truth state that Adam is a group of beings, not just one who lived in the etheric counterpart of Earth and eventually divided into male and female. Eden was not physically on earth; it is a paradise. The Adams originated from seven billion incarnated souls and, at that time, it was impossible for every human to come to earth at the same time.

The book of Enoch in the Bible describes how a group of two hundred beings from the sky decided to interbreed with humanity. Their leader Semjaza became worried because he was afraid he would get the blame if they were found out. To reassure him, the group met together on Mount Hermon and swore to accept collective responsibility. They then put the plan into action. When the matters went badly wrong, the worsening situation was reported back to God who put a stop to the whole sorry business with the deluge, sparing only Noah and his kin and animals.

Eden in the Sumerian creation story was much the same as the biblical account but told in an opposite way. Sumerian culture existed five thousand years ago and one thousand years before Jewish culture came into existence. Eve's counterpart in the Sumerian story is given an apple from the tree but, in this story, the tree is upside down meaning it has its roots in heaven and, by the woman giving the man the apple, she is giving him nourishment from this cosmic tree.

In the Sumerian story, the woman is held in high regard as opposed to Eve being the temptress. The snake in ancient societies was seen as a symbol of eternity and renewal as it shed its old skin and regenerated with a new one. But where did we begin from before our incarnation? I searched for this answer for many, many years of my life, and it's my belief the man who was the greatest Christian mystic and healer of the 20th century had the ability to go back to the beginning of time and explore the cosmic consciousness through examatosis.

His name was Dr. Stylianos Atteshlis also known as Daskalos. He was the founder of the Researchers of Truth. I studied his work in the various books he published, the meditational CDs of his daughter, Panayiota Atteshli, and read a book about Daskalos called *Fire in the Heart*.

The term monad comes from the Greek Mystery Schools. Pythagoras created the symbol for it: a circle with a dot in the middle (**8**). The black dot represents the incomprehensible part of us, that eternal Spirit Being. A monad is like a cell within the body of God. Each monad emanates streams of pure life light. These rays are eternal spirit beings but they are not yet human beings. According to the plan, some of these rays are destined to be humanised. They pass through the archetype, the Human Idea, at which point our soul is created. Pythagoras called this symbol a holy little number.

From the Australian Aboriginal perspective, they don't believe life begins during the act of reproduction. Many tribal groups believe the baby may enter the egg days or weeks later at a specific dreaming place and the female will travel to that place to receive her child.

In a TV series, *Learn Indigenous Australian Creation Stories: Song Lines on the Screen*, the story is told about the Dreaming place at Keep River National Park in the Northern Territory, where women can go to become pregnant. Researchers of the Truth and Aboriginal thinking are near identical when it comes to understanding conception.

Researchers of Truth are aware that when a soul is ready for a new incarnation, the Spirit Ray Soul descends and we stop for a period in the psychical plane. The incarnating soul has to wait until there are appropriate conditions prepared on Earth so that the ray of the spirit soul enters the body of a newborn. We are born but for what purpose?

Edgar Cayce's Association for Research and Enlightenment may help answer some of those questions. A reading states that God desires to be expressed in the world through us. The example set by Jesus is the "pattern" of wholeness for each soul. It could be said he is the blueprint who has been given to us so we may follow. After all, he said, "I am the Way, the Truth and the Light."

From our abode at the caravan park on the Johnston River, Ryan and I moved to a high blockhouse a little further up the river. We also took in a boarder who, in the end, took our money and ran. There was something strange about that house, so we only stayed about six months. Our next move was to Walnut Street right next door to a good friend. I continued my work at Kool FM on a part-time basis and continued as a sole parent.

As the three boys and I found new swimming holes and places to camp all across North Queensland, we more or less stumbled upon a white pyramid. On further investigation, we found out that it was a house built just like a pyramid and painted white. It had windows but the rest of it for all intents and purposes, was a pyramid. Being white, it could be seen from up to 20 km away on a clear day. We found out it was built by a pyramid fanatic by the name of Pyramid Pete. The population of North Queensland still has a good sense of humor.

We drove up to it one day as curiosity got the better of me. I took a couple of photos of it. It still stands today shining like a beacon on a summer's day, still visible from most parts of the Johnston

Shire. From the vision of a white pyramid in Deniliquin, the pieces were finally starting to fit.

I also experienced another vision at this time. I was given sacred numbers of 24.3. It would take another fifteen years to figure that one out but in the meantime I was happy I'd found the white pyramid that I'd seen so clearly in vision state in Deniliquin. "Awakening in himself it is possible for someone to become the master of materialisation, able to materialise objects on the three-dimensional plane from the other planes," the statement was now also about to become a reality.

I don't know what the catalyst was for it or even how it actually began but I found myself thinking something and it would actually happen. I would go down to a reasonably fast flowing creek and I would see a branch of a tree floating down it. I would put my mind into it and ask for it to come right to where I was on the bank. Since this can be could have been a coincidence, I tried it again. I pushed the log out into the creek, it floated down past the point of no return, and again with my mind, I brought it right to my feet. I did the whole thing again and sure enough, the log came back.

Here I was again with the awakening of my real self, being able to do things many would think impossible. However, I was again feeling unable to share any of this with anyone.

The next incident was a get together with neighbours. There were about seven of us who were all gathered in the shade of the trees in the backyard. Our drinks consisted of either water or soft drinks. There was no alcohol. I began to understand what this awakening meant and I suggested to one of the women that she was actually drinking rum and coke. Sure enough, she agreed with me. In fact, she went one step further and started to act in a drunken manner.

I told the next woman that she was drinking vodka and orange juice and the same thing happened to her. Before I knew it, the whole table was acting as though everyone had been drinking loads of alcohol. Soon, all of the adults at the table were acting very drunk. This party continued into the night. We put a barbecue together and partied on soft drinks and water for around nine hours. Ryan, who was nine at the time, can vouch for the out-of-control party on water and soft drinks.

One day when he feels ready, Ryan has an even more amazing story to tell from that night regarding a crocodile. However, I'll wait until he's ready to share that story. At that stage, I was having the other two boys over to Walnut Street every second weekend and Ryan would stay with his mum every other weekend. He had made some good friends. Even the adults took a liking to him. He continued this tradition all through his years of growing up.

The Christ Consciousness was awakening in a far stronger force than ever before. Everything around me seemed to come alive. I was reading volumes and volumes of books on esoteric subjects. I read a lot on Edgar Cayce. I even put his book under my pillow but I didn't get his same results. Nevertheless, he was a guiding light. He made clear that the transformative power of the Christ Consciousness is awakened as individuals act in accordance with the pattern set by the example of Jesus' life.

From Cayce's perspective, Jesus is the Elder Brother for all humankind, deeply committed to assisting all souls in reawakening to the awareness of their oneness with God. The more I believed the more seemingly miraculous things began to occur. I already had a fair list that I couldn't explain to anyone. Therefore, what did it matter if I added one more? As my vibration changed and my belief deepened, I knew anything on planet Earth was possible and I went to new heights on a regular basis.

There was something deep inside me that wanted to come out. I knew my body was getting lighter. I could just feel it. I got out of bed and got to work on testing my theory that my body had dematerialised. I picked up a long clap stick that a close friend gave me (clapsticks are a type of drumstick or percussion mallet that serve to maintain rhythm in Aboriginal voice chants) (and I passed this piece of wood through one leg and then the next. I did this a number of times and the same thing happened every time. I expected to feel the wood as it started to go through my flesh but my leg stayed intact and the wood passed through.

It would be several years before I could validate what had happened. The world of science was able to prove to me what happened certainly was possible, if a person learns how to vibrate at a certain frequency. Science tells us an atom has a nucleus and electrons orbiting around it. It consists of 1% matter and 99% empty space. The atom's nucleus is equivalent to a speck of dust in the centre of a sports arena with the electron orbiting around it.

When Christ and Peter walked upon the water in the Lake of Galilee, they more than likely dematerialised both their bodies. Peter only managed it for a short while but for me the moral to the story is that he did do it and Christ was showing us we could all do it. We can do as Peter did: dematerialise our body and walk on water. The Aboriginal Clever Men (Magic Men) of Australia have been doing these sorts of things for over 60,000 years. The shamans of other countries have also been doing the same thing.

During his first voyage in 1492, Columbus reached the New World, landing on an island in the Bahamas Archipelago that he named San Salvador. When the ships of Columbus appeared on the horizon, the natives couldn't physically see them. It took the shaman to notice (although he didn't see them at first; he just noticed the water moving differently until one day he actually saw the ships). This is when the shaman told his people about the ships before they could actually perceive them. "You have to believe it before you can see it" is a mantra that explains these phenomena.

In addition to my part-time sales job at Kool FM, I was also now doing a gig with the breakfast presenter, Ruth. It was a very crazy segment, pushing all of the boundaries left and right, so much that the manager was quite often on my back. Ruth was just outright fun and we put together one of the best gigs with which I have been associated as a duo in my radio career.

There was so much going on for me spiritually, that I was having trouble sleeping. One night, I got in the car and drove about 20 km. I can remember the night very clearly, even though it was nearly two decades ago. As I got to the junction of the road that leads from Currajah to the Tablelands, I could see a massive pure white horse up ahead in a paddock on the corner. I pulled the car up, parked, and went over to the fence to talk to this magnificent animal. It was beyond magnificent. It was about twice the size of a normal horse. This was a spirit horse. I knew that because as it reared up its back feet, they weren't on the ground. This spirit horse was suspended in the air and the wind was blowing across its mane and tail.

Regardless of whether it was spirit or not, I felt I knew this horse and tried to talk to it. I asked it to come to the fence and talk to me. However, he was beyond this world. I would find out much later that the white horse in symbology is very, very powerful. I was relieved some years later when I was able to find an explanation for the white horse from Edgar Cayce who said in his book *From the Book of Revelation*, that the white horse is the symbol of the messenger in the awakening. The messenger is Jesus Christ.

It's this significant event in my life that has led me to name this book *The White Horse & The Wandjina*. I can still see the magnificent animal and if called upon, I could drive right to that very same spot where I saw him that day. One day, when I'm on the other side, I believe that I'll have a chance to ride him.

I drove home with this incredible feeling welling up inside of me. It was a feeling that I had never felt before. It's as if it came from a deep well and came gushing to the top and I cried out "I am!" You wanted me to say it; now I've said it. I'll say it once more just in case you missed it: I am! From there on, there was no holding back. Tears flowed down my cheeks, but they were happy tears. They were tears of release and they represented so much of what I'd held back for so long, because I was afraid to say those two words. My drive home was blissful. I felt at peace.

White horses have a special significance in the mythologies of cultures around the world. The white horse is a symbol for developing awareness of your instincts and intuition. The Purana scriptures foretell that Kalki, the tenth incarnation of Vishnu and final world saviour, is predicted to return atop a white horse with a drawn blazing sword.

They are often associated with the sun chariot, warrior heroes and fertility (in both mare and stallion manifestations). They all have an end-of-time saviour. However, other interpretations also exist. From the earliest times, white horses have been mythologised as possessing exceptional properties and transcending the normal world by having wings (e.g. Pegasus from Greek mythology). As part of its legendary dimension, the white horse in myth may be depicted with seven heads. There are also white horses which are divinatory and who prophesize or warn of danger.

In Celtic mythology, Rhiannon, a mythic figure, rides a pale white horse. In Norse mythology, Odin's eight-legged horse, Sleipnir, is described as the best horse among gods and men. In Zoroastrianism, a white horse appears again and white horses appear many times in Hindu mythology. The Vedic horse sacrifice of Ashvamedha was a fertility and kinship ritual involving the sacrifice of a white stallion. Similar rituals may have taken place among Roman, Celtic, and Norse people.

Kanthaka was a white horse that was a royal servant and a favourite horse of Prince Siddhartha, who later became Gautama Buddha. Some Christian saints are associated with white steeds: St James, as patron saint of Spain, rides a white horse in his martial aspect. St George, the patron saint of horsemen, among other things, also rides a white horse. Twelver Shi'a is Madhi tradition envisage that the Mahdi will appear riding a white horse.

It seems that wherever I look in symbology and mythology there's a white horse. The Korean city of Pangantucan, has as its symbol a white stallion that saved the ancient tribes from being massacred by uprooting a bamboo and thus warning them of the enemy's approach. The city of Hanoi has a white horse as its patron saint and last, but not least, from the *Book of Revelation*: "And I saw when the Lamb opened one of the seals, and I heard, as it were the noise of thunder, one of the four beasts saying, 'Come and see.' And I saw, and beheld a white horse: and he that sat on him had a bow; and a crown was given unto him: and he went forth conquering." (Revelation 6:1-2)

A special friend from the Blue Mountains sent me the book by Edgar Cayce that would help me to understand the white horse.

White horse or no white horse, I had to go to work to make a living while all of this was happening around me. During this period in my life, I was consistently in a raised state of consciousness and at times, I was brushing the edges of Oneness.

At around the same time, I became interested in a lady that lived in Cairns. Ryan and I would occasionally travel there to visit her and her two girls.

My level of consciousness had risen to heights I'd never experienced before. However, my erratic sleeping patterns and my everyday communication skills were declining. Ryan was starting to feel ill at ease living with me, so he asked to go back and live with his mum and two brothers. It saddened me to see him go because I felt we had a special bond and had shared great adventures. However, I was thankful for the times we had together and so I moved on. Some months after Ryan had moved back with his mum, I moved to Cairns.

One of the first things I noticed upon my arrival in Cairns was a massive triangle etched into the rock of what is known as the Lamb Ranges. These mountains were very impressive. I could see this triangle every time I looked towards the west or was driving a car going to my home. The actual triangle was of a white colour and was much more splendid in the morning hours, especially around 7 AM to 9 AM. It looked like one side of the pyramid I'd seen in a vision in Deniliquin. I had then actually found it at a little place called Garradunga. It was the white pyramid that Pete had built. The triangle on the mountain was caused by erosion that just so happened to form the shape of a pyramid. Seven years later, I would encounter small white pyramids in a caravan park that I stayed in.

In the meantime, hardly a day went by that I didn't connect with that white pyramid on the side of the mountain. Seventeen years later, the white triangle on the mountain is all but gone. Vegetation has reclaimed and covered up what was once my white pyramid. It is possible to see a little bit of what it looked like for around 15 minutes in the morning, at approximately 7:15 AM when the sun is shining brightly. After that, it really claims the secret it once held.

I was only in Cairns for a month, when I scanned the radio dial and heard this station that was playing indigenous music. Like a moth to the flame, I was soon in the office discussing a volunteer position. I had never before heard an indigenous radio station anywhere in Australia. With my connection to the indigenous spirit world, I could feel that something would come of it. After a couple of months as a volunteer, I was offered the job as Senior Broadcaster at radio BBM Cairns.

The CEO described my two months as Breakfast Presenter to the board and they agreed to take me on. The CEO, the senior broadcaster, and I sat down with a coffee and within half an hour, we came up with a winning formula for a new station sound. Three months later, it was spreading throughout Cairns like a fire in Central Queensland in the middle of December. It was possible to get into half the cabs in Cairns and they would have 98.7 FM blaring out of the radio speaker.

Before my engagement at BBM, the station had been taking a Brisbane station on relay to Cairns. It wasn't too long before talk got around that BBM 98.7 FM had a new kid on the block that was really worthlistening to. Indigenous people were listening and non-indigenous people turned the dial to 98.7 FM. Most were aware that it was an indigenous radio station. However, for many months, they didn't tell their friends about it. It was simply because we were a Black Radio Station. But like any good secret, it's too good to hold on to. Within twelve months, BBM

98.7 FM was blaring out of shops, homes, cars, and worksites. A healing was going on, silently, effectively, and lastingly.

One morning, I made a comment about man's lust for gold as I referred to a song by Dan Fogelberg. Whatever I said, offended a listener and he phoned to rant and rave about his granddad mining gold in the Palmer River. I couldn't really argue back as we were always trained to be courteous under all circumstances to our clients, our audience, and the public in general.

I may have been courteous but underneath I was simmering. He was one of the rudest human beings I had ever encountered. I thought to myself if I was doing *Talkback*, I could make mincemeat out of him. He set a chain in motion and I actively started to pursue the idea of talkback radio.

While I had my mind set on talkback radio, the spirit was ready to become manifest once more. It was 1999, just after 5 AM in the morning when I was driving down Spence Street in Cairns. Now, like my very first vision, I was driving a car and at the same time conscious of the vision happening simultaneously.

This time as I drove the car, the street was lined with thousands and thousands of people all dressed up, happy, cheering and waving at me. At the end of the line were the king and queen and all their royal subjects and even the king and queen were clapping and cheering. I made a left turn into Abbott Street and left the crowd behind. I got out of my car and went about my work as if nothing had happened. I did my normal breakfast program and as usual, I told no one. The visions now seemed a part of everyday life. This statement now started to have meaning for me, "Dreams, visions, signs, intuition, and significant events will steer you towards making necessary changes in your life."

I also received help from the Spiritual Emergency Network. They have done research into visions, hearing voices, and similar things. They have also found that nearly one in seven persons hear voices, see visions, or have other forms of sensory experience which others do not. Some of their research indicates that an overwhelming majority of people have some form of spiritual, mystical, or visionary experience in their lifetimes. This vision was the precursor to the biggest indigenous talkback radio program Australia had ever seen.

Working at BBM, gave me the opportunity to connect with the indigenous people that I so longed to do. This yearning to know more and be around indigenous people was finally being fulfilled. It was a big year because it's when we went from a temporary broadcasting license to receiving our full-time license on 1 April 1999. We were finally legitimate.

My initial reason for coming to Cairns, after Ryan had gone back to his mum's, was to move in with the lady from Norway and her two daughters. She was very receptive to indigenous culture, having come from a country where the culture went all the way back to the Vikings. She was a good woman and helped me topursue my career. My three sons didn't share the same opinion. As a result, their planned visits every second weekend became increasingly difficult.

I did a lot of driving over that period. I drove down to Innisfail, picked the boys up and then drove back to Cairns. We spent a weekend in Cairns and then back to Innisfail to drop the boys off and then drove back to Cairns. It wasn't a good period. Resentment started to grow between the boys, the lady and her daughters. I stood in the middle trying to be a peacemaker but to no avail.

2000 was the year of the Olympics and Cathy Freeman was set for the 400m. *The National Indigenous Radio Service* approached me to see if I wanted to be part of their Olympics broadcast team, even though I was not indigenous. I didn't have to think too long. The next thing I knew, I was stepping out of the plane into the madness of Sydney airport.

The Chairman of the *National Indigenous Radio Service* picked me up at the airport. It was time to get acquainted with the equipment and to learn Windows 98. How could I forget? I had only operated a computer a couple of times before in my life. My lack of computer skills didn't hold me back and I managed to secure some really top-rated interviews.

We had a great team. There was a great group of elders that accompanied some of the remote communities who we relied on for guidance. They seemed unflustered by all the events happening around them. A full 24 hours before the big race, they announced that Cathy had won. There was no fanfare and no fuss. There was just that simple statement. When the race was actually on, we all kind of felt that we already knew the outcome. Cathy brought home the bacon. She proudly carried the indigenous flag all around the track. Indigenous people, with whom I've spoken over the years, list that as one of their most treasured memories.

Many white Australians started to rethink and rebuild their relationships with Black Australia because Cathy belonged to all of Australia. In the Olympic village, we found the big marquee that acted as the bookshop for indigenous writers. Stock was going out at an incredible pace. Cathy really was the flavour of the 2000 Olympics.

I was so thrilled to see David Mowaljarlai's book *Yorro Yorro* available for sale. Yorro Yorro means "As it is above so it is below" and that being the case, I guess the angels in heaven were dancing over Cathy's win. I finally got the opportunity to talk to the manager of the National Indigenous Radio Service. I asked him if it would be possible to start a talkback program on the National Indigenous Radio Service. He replied, "When would you like to start?" I said, "As soon as possible if that's all right with you," and so it was.

The Olympics were ending. I made some really great friends and had a really incredible time. When going home, I knew that I was going to embark upon the biggest move in my radio career. I could just feel it in the water. It took about three months to get extra phone lines put on and the infrastructure purchased and installed.

I don't remember the exact date but I'm pretty sure it was July when we launched *TalkBlack*. The very first guest on the program was Terry O'Shane, who was the head of the local Aboriginal controlled organisation called ATSIC. Everything went according to plan: the interview was good and it was the beginning of seven years of incredible radio from the studios of BBM.

We started out with just three stations taking the broadcast including: Cairns, Townsville, and Rockhampton. There weren't many calls to start with, so I filled the blank spaces with news items and anything connected with indigenous culture. We were presenting something brand new, something that had never been attempted before in the way we were doing it. The days, weeks, and months rolled on and the calls started to come. One of my first real testing calls was between two different tribal groups that had an altercation at a local football carnival. I became a peacemaker and managed to get both groups to agree to a peace treaty. It was the first of many such calls that would come over the years.

More people started phoning in, more stations heard about it and joined and, eventually, fifty-three indigenous stations ended up receiving the broadcast from 3KND in the South, right to the very top of Australia to Bamaga, Injinoo, New Mapoon, and Seisia and across to Darwin in NT and Broome and Derby in WA.

The program became so popular that we had to install an extra phone line and, in addition, we needed someone to produce the program as well as having me in the broadcast chair. At our peak, we took sixteen calls in an hour and managed to fit in a little music as well. That was less than four minutes per call to fit them all into the hour that we had available to broadcast.

After I had returned from the 2000 Olympics and our broadcast on the National Indigenous Radio Service, I did an interview with a very prominent indigenous woman who was head of the Australian Museum in Sydney. At the end of the interview, she asked me if I would like to go to Guangzhou with the large exhibition. In fact, it was one of the biggest art exhibitions ever to leave the shores of this country. I'm not sure if she knew that I wasn't Aboriginal, but I didn't make an issue of it. She'd asked me and I accepted.

The gallery showcased a selection of the Museum's 40,000-piece collection of Indigenous Australian tools, artworks, adornments, and other cultural materials acquired from early European settlement to the present. Combined with audiovisual, storytelling, and personal narratives, the gallery's aim was to capture the diversity of Aboriginal and Torres Strait Islander art and culture from the Dreaming to the present day. We were taking to Guangzhou one of the biggest collections of Aboriginal and Torres Strait Islander art ever to leave this country. What was the biggest buzz for me, was the inclusion of the Wandjina art from the Kimberley. When I saw it up there on the wall in all its glory in China, I somehow felt a little bit of me was there as well.

I'd never been overseas before and a long flight to Guangzhou was not exactly my idea of fun. We got the passport and visas organised, and as I went to board my flight, the attendant asked me, "Would you like to fly business class? That's a really nice shirt you're wearing." It didn't take too long to figure that one out.

The trip was okay but going through customs turned into a bit of a nightmare. I've worn an Akubra hat for many years. It was right on top of my head as I attempted to go through the scanner at customs. The alarm went off at least four times that I can remember. I was starting to get pretty jumpy and so were the custom officers who looked more like they came out of the army than customs. It seemed quite possible I would be detained if I couldn't come up with something plausible. Then it dawned on me that the hat had a little hat pin on it. I handed it to the customs guy and then went through. Greg Reid was officially welcomed to China, carrying hat in hand.

The next thing that really set me back was the scene of beggars outside the doors at the airport. I'd never seen this before. We were instructed to give them nothing as our group was hurried into cars. We were taken to a very up-market hotel, the flashiest I'd ever been in, and we checked in.

I was only there 24 hours, when I came down with what is called "Bali Water." I was so dehydrated that they had to put me into a hospital and give me a drip. When a Chinese doctor became available, he felt around with his hand on my stomach. I felt an incredible pain when he touched the area. I'm not sure whether he actually inserted his hand like a traditional healer or just pushed in very hard. I was in so much pain, I didn't dare to look.

I was in the hospital for three days and missed much of our purpose of being there. However, I did get out to view the city a couple of times when, unfortunately, Guangzhou was bathed in heavily polluted smog. It was so bad that I could barely breathe. I had to go to the doctor again to obtain medication for asthma brought on by the pollution. I've never seen anything like it in my life. The art exhibition was accompanied by dancers from Saibai Island. They were wonderful ambassadors for their homeland.

The place where Aboriginal culture and China came together was at the Hard Rock Cafe. This was where the dancers unwound at night. Most Chinese had never seen a black person before, so Chinese patrons would give the Torres Strait Island dancers free drinks. The only problem was that the Hard Rock Cafe stayed open until late at night and the dancers would be late for their performances the next day.

It came time to say our goodbyes to Guangzhou, pack our bags and head home. It was a seven-hour flight to Melbourne. As we about to take off, five Asian men sat next to me. After we ascended and were in full flight, they all got up and found other seats. I am not sure if I had BO or they simply wanted to sit somewhere else, but the good news was I had six seats in the middle. If I put the armrests up on all of them, I could make myself a good place to sleep.

I slept until it was half an hour out from landing. We got a connecting flight to Sydney. I then had to find a way to ground myself since flying upsets my equilibrium. I walked around and around a park in Sydney trying to orientate myself for almost three hours. After that, I figured out where I was.

The manager of BBM, Ken Reys, had filled in doing *TalkBlack* while I was away in China. Upon my return, it was back behind the microphone again. More stations joined our network and the callers grew in number every day.

Numbers started to come to me in meditations and visions. This was eating away at me. I wanted to see the light of day, so I decided to have the measurements that I saw in my visions made up into a small, stainless steel pyramid rod. I had this made at a local engineering works but I didn't know what to do with it. I tried all kinds of things, but it didn't seem to have a purpose. Eventually, I discarded it into a dying part of the garden. Two weeks later, I walked past this part of the garden and noticed that the plants had received a new lease of life. I thought this might just be a coincidence, so I put the pyramid over another plant that was dying. The same thing happened as before: the plant fully recovered to its former glory. I just had to do it one more time and the same thing occurred. The plant fully recovered.

There are many other applications for which it could be used. I just haven't managed to get a patent registered. Other things in life have always seemed to have precedence over my precious pyramid. However, there will come a time when I will work on it and see it through to its fullest potential.

I was a smoker back then and quite often went downstairs to sit on a bench next to the Abbott Street to have a cigarette. One afternoon while I was having a puff, a man and his wife from North East Arnhem Land walked by. He later told me that he said these words to his wife, "I'm going to adopt him into our culture." Well, it didn't happen immediately. However, about twelve months later, I finally got to meet Maylia Wunungmurra and his wife Sheryl. He didn't tell me what was going on. He just asked me to have a meal with him and his family. Over time, we grew closer and he told me more and more sacred things from his world.

I clearly remember having a barbecue at our place one day. For whatever reason, we decided to do an impromptu rain dance. I followed Maylia's lead. Much to my amazement, on a summer's day with a clear blue sky, it started to rain. It rained a decent amount as well without a cloud. I was starting to see into a world I never knew existed before. I learned how to play the clapsticks and listen for that particular beat. I would later learn that clapsticks, when played in a particular way, could take a group or an individual to a heightened state of consciousness.

Maylia was from the Dhalwangu language area of the Yolgnu Nation and his moiety group was the Yirritja. Given time, this is what I would become. I would also have a new name: Dharayara Wunungmurra. Dharayara was a name that meant sacred tree and tallest in the forest. I would later learn upon my adopted father's death, the significance of the name that was bequeathed to me. I would eventually meet up with Maylia's dad, Yanggariny, when my then partner and I invited him for dinner one night at our house in Brinsmead.

On this night, I would finally find out about the power of a Law man. The law was passed down generation to generation and not necessarily father to son. It could be bestowed from grandfather to grandson. These laws can't be changed or altered like Western society changes its laws. It is rock solid from day one and stays rock solid forever. Many sacred objects are also passed on to whoever receives the law at the time of the lawman's death.

Maylia, his father, his wife, his son, daughter and adopted daughter all came for the night. I had no idea what was about to happen. You don't read about this kind of thing in books. It is something that you feel and something you know.

We all sat outside on the veranda and had drinks and some nibbles. There was small talk, like there usually is at these kinds of get-togethers. At that point, I had consumed one light stubby of beer. Then it hit me. I could feel that Yanggariny was reading me, every thought and everything in my heart and mind. As a result, I became afraid. He wasn't even looking at me but I knew exactly what was going on. It was so powerful that I thought I was going to fall off my chair because I was so dizzy. It couldn't be the beer because I'd only had one light beer for the whole afternoon. But undoubtedly, he was reading me like an x-ray. I found it difficult to talk to him for the rest of the night, just in case I said something out of line.

We had an excellent dinner, aside from the fact that I had just had every inch of my body surveyed by someone who could read my mind. This was scary stuff since I didn't know anyone existed like this on planet Earth. The dinner concluded and everyone left happy. They drove down the driveway and while all of this was taking place, Yanggariny said to Maylia, "He'll have my last name."

Maylia informed me of this at our next meeting. I was now officially Dharayara Wunungmurra, of the Yirritja moiety, of the Dhalwangu tribe, of the Yolngu Nation. I don't use my Aboriginal name publicly or on the radio where it would've been easy to do so. Today, the same mystery still surrounds me. There are many radio listeners where I work who are convinced that I'm of Aboriginal descent.

The workings of Aboriginal culture are very complex. As a result, I have only learned a small proportion of what is possible to learn. In Yolgnu, a man can have up to five names. They are all used in different ways for different purposes. Some are used solely in sacred men's business and are never uttered outside of the circle. With a sacred name, even the children of that parent may not know that name until it comes time close to death.

Dharayara was one of Yanggariny's inside sacred names, not even Maylia was aware of that until he was close to death. I have revered the name, known to only a few before I wrote this book. When Maylia greets me, it is this name that he uses. But this was only the start. I was to be privy to much, much more over the years.

In time, I would visit the homeland called Gan Gan which was 300 km southwest of Nhulunbuy on a dirt road. When it was wet, the only way in was via a small plane. I was invited to attend a very special ceremony called the Initiation Ceremony at Gan Gan with Maylia and his family. We flew to Nhulunbuy and then to Gan Gan where we were greeted enthusiastically by Maylia's family. It was a decent walk from the airstrip to our new home for a couple of weeks.

Gan Gan is steeped in history. It is where Baramah (the creation ancestor) rose up out of the water hole and with the water glistening on the diamond shapes on his body, he set out and gave law to all North East Arnhem Land. The waterhole is so sacred the local people don't swim in it.

Yolngu culture is based on a strong sense of connection to land and sea. Yirrkala is ancestral land belonging to the Rirratjingu language area. Yolngu have traded and intermarried with Macassans since c.1100-1600 AD. In 1935, when the Federal Government was considering a punitive expedition (massacre) against the Yolngu, Mawalan Marika invited the missionary Wilbur Chaseling to establish a mission at Yirrkala.

In the following years, the leadership of the Yolngu resisted their dispossession by the government, missionaries, a potential Japanese invasion and Bauxite miners. In addition to the Yirrkala Church Panels and the Yirrkala Bark Petition, they have used their art to assert their connection to land in the Government Land Rights Case, the Woodward Royal Commission, the Barunga Statement, the Yirrkala Homeland Movement, the Land Rights Act (NT) 1976, the Both Ways education bilingual curriculum, and the world-renowned contemporary music band Yothu Yindi.

Under Yolngu Law, the Land extends to include the sea. Both land and sea are connected in a single cycle of life for which the Yolngu hold the songs and designs. To demonstrate their rights and responsibilities over specific areas of coast and sea and to protect those same marine environments from abuse by outsiders, the landowners combined to make the Saltwater Collection of Yirrkala Bark Paintings of Sea Country in 1997. The Collection of 80 bark paintings made by forty-seven Yolngu artists is featured in a publication of the same name.

CHAPTER 5

GAN GAN NT

In my opinion, North East Arnhem Land is some of the most special country there is in this vast great land we call Australia. Visitors must obtain a permit to enter from the Land Council.

I was about to learn what a controlled state of altered consciousness is all about. I was in Gan Gan with my adopted brother, his wife and family. I was about to undergo the greatest learning experience in my life. I had been exposed to indigenous people my entire life, but the Yolngu had not been affected by white invasion like the rest of Australia. English was their second language and in some groups it was their fourth or fifth. They spoke in the mother tongue Yolngu and then alternated with one of the fifteen or sixteen dialects associated with the mother tongue.

I felt like I'd parachuted into the middle of Germany, since I didn't understand any of the languages and only a very limited amount of English was spoken. I was now the outsider in what I thought was my own country. It was easy to see that these people were the true custodians of this country. They had lived anywhere from 60,000 to 100,000 years in an unbroken line. Theirs and other remaining tribal nations in Australia made up the longest surviving religion in the world. I was in the middle of nowhere, learning to observe body language and a new language.

I was welcome as anyone could be. I was treated like royalty. I felt at peace in a way that I've never felt before. We came for ceremony and on Day Two, the dig (didgeridoo) and the clap sticks called out to the spirits. The drone of the dig and rhythm of the clap sticks would not stop for nearly a week. Every day, we asked when the ceremony was going to be and the answer every day was, "today."

The singers started to join the drone of the dig mid-afternoon and they would go well into the night. The next day it was the same and it was the same the following day. What I didn't realise at the time, was that the drone of the didgeridoo accompanied by the clap sticks and singing of sacred songs raised everyone's state of consciousness in the community. As each day went on, the level of consciousness rose and we were all in a semi-hypnotic state.

I was allowed to record much of the ceremony, except for the sacred songs. It was my understanding this was the first time the recording of the ceremony had been allowed. I still have a copy of it on my hard drive in my computer.

Maylia's son was chosen for this initiation ceremony and since part of that ceremony involved his manhood; he was understandably a little on edge. I would take him and the other children down to the river just above whereby Baramah rose up out of the water hole. We would spend many hours swimming and having fun. No one asked me to do this. I just could feel this is what the elders would want me to do.

All Yolngu people in North East Arnhem Land belong to one of two basic divisions, or moieties, called Dhuwa and Yirritja. Children belong to the same moiety as their father; their mother belongs to the other moiety.

Everything in the Yolngu universe: spirit beings, plant and animal species, clan groups and areas of land and water are either Dhuwa or Yirritja. The Djang'kawu Sisters, the morning star, the water goanna, the stringybark tree, and the land in and around Yirrkala are Dhuwa, while such things as the evening star, stingray, cycad palm, and members of the Mangalili clan are all Yirritja.

Within each moiety, people belong to smaller groups called clans, each having its own language. Children belong to their father's clan and moiety, while their mother belongs to another clan of the other moiety. In the Gove Peninsula and the surrounding area, most Yolngu belong to one of sixteen clans, of which eight are Dhuwa and eight are Yirritja.

In my first swim in the river, I laid back and felt this is the life. Right at that point, I heard a voice within say, "Welcome home." The water under me at that point felt like silk and satin and I was held up semi-suspended in the water. In one of my other lifetimes, this must have been my homeland and I was being welcomed back home.

The Yolngu people had trading contact with Macassans from Indonesia for at least six hundred years prior to the arrival of the Europeans. In return for the Yolngu allowing them to gather pearls and trepang, the Macassans provided the Yolngu with various goods including knives, canoes, metal, tobacco, and pipes.

For the Yolngu people, culture is a manifestation of their ties to the land and the supernatural world that resides there. The focus of the spiritual life of the Aboriginal people is the Dreaming, which is a reality beyond the everyday world. It is a reality that brings moral order to the cosmos. Through stories of supernatural beings and ancestors that lived long ago, the

Aboriginal peoples learn how the laws of social and religious behaviour came about and, more importantly, how to maintain harmony between humans and the natural universe.

The stories of the Dreaming are sometimes widespread but more often regional and even residing in individual families. Individuals often inherit rights to depict specific Dreaming stories and to communicate the religious meaning of those stories to the world at large. With the subjugation of the Aboriginal peoples by European colonizers beginning in 1788, and the recent rejuvenation of Aboriginal culture and civil rights, there has been a resurgence of pride and interest in the stories of the Dreaming. The Yolngu people in their art, music, and dance have been prominent in this Aboriginal cultural renaissance. There is evidence of rock paintings in Arnhem Land from as early as 50,000 years ago.

Maylia's son, who was the centre of attention in this ceremony, was being painted up on his stomach and chest in a sacred design connected to his mother's country. This painting took two days to complete. By the time the painting had been completed, the young lad was in an altered state of consciousness. There were no drugs and only the sound of didgeridoo, clap sticks, and sacred songs. His eyes were glazed over and he was ready for the ceremony to begin. He also wore special armbands made out of rainbow lorikeet feathers and another band around his head that had possum skin attached to it and a tail that ran down his back.

These sacred objects took hundreds of hours to make and have been passed down from generation to generation. Special dances were performed and eventually part of his manhood was removed with no anesthetic, just a very sharp scalpel. He then was ushered away to where a group of women had lit a very special fire whose smoke would help heal the recently acquired wound.

Some people would query the purpose of this practice, but I saw with my very own eyes the very specific reason that a young man is put through this kind of ceremony. 300 km from the nearest town is a long distance to hike if a young lad became fearful and wanted to run. There is just bush and more bush. By the time his turn comes around for ceremony, he has surrendered, his fear has gone and he is prepared to face the knife. Fear in an initiation ceremony is based on a young man's manhood and removing the very end part. The strangest part of it all is that part of a man's manhood has very few nerves and blood vessels. In fact, the pain isn't much different from getting your ears pierced. However, 99 out of 100 men are fearful of losing that part of their manhood, simply because they don't know the full story and the lack of pain involved.

This is the way most fear is when imagined. It's not real and is not in proportion to the danger. Once a young man or boy has overcome this great fear early in his life, there is not too much more in life of which he will be fearful. He will walk differently, will be self-assured and will act differently because he knows who he is. In an ever-changing world where men at times struggle with their identity and their purpose in a modern world, I would advocate that each young boy take a similar journey early in their life.

I felt honoured to witness what I saw over the two weeks that I was in the community. I was treated like a king at every mealtime and we ate much of what came off the land. There was kangaroo that was cooked in a pit underground, goanna, brolga, file snake, fish, rainbow lorikeets, turtle and yam and the women of the camp constantly made damper.

The complete system of Yolngu law is known as the Maḏayin. Maḏayin embodies the rights of the owners of the law, or citizens (rom watangu walal) who have the rights and responsibilities for this embodiment of law. Maḏayin includes all the people's law (rom); the instruments and objects that encode and symbolise the law (Maḏayin girri'); oral dictates; names and song cycles; and the holy, restricted places (dhuyu ṉuŋgat wäṉa) that are used in the maintenance, education, and development of law.

Yolngu use hollow logs in traditional burial rituals. They are also an important "canvas" for their art. This law covers the ownership of land and waters, the resources on or within these lands and waters. It regulates and controls production and trade, and the moral, social and religious law including laws for the conservation and farming of plants and aquatic life.

Gan Gan Outstation, which lies north-west of Blue Mud Bay in Eastern Arnhem Land, is the homeland of the Dhalwangu people and the most sacred site of the Yolngu Yirritja moiety. Barama, the great creator ancestor and lawgiver of the Yirritja, came upriver from Blue Mud Bay, emerging at a freshwater site known as Gulutji. It was at this site that he called together a council of Dhalwangu elders and sent off two, Lany'tjung and Galparimun, to Gan Gan Outstation, which lies northwest of Blue Mud Bay in East Arnhem Land, to the give the law to all Yirritja people. This story is the Yirritja equivalent to the great and better known, Dhuwa creation myth of the Djang'kawu Sisters, which begins on the beach at Yalangbara, just to the south of Yirrkala.

I met Maylia's dad, his many brothers, sisters, brothers-in-law, sisters-in-laws, nieces, nephews and cousins. I eventually met everyone that lived in the community, including Dr Gawirrin Gumana, lawman, and the most respected leader in all of Arnhem Land. Gawirrin had leprosy as a child and lost many of his fingers on both hands. What were left were just stubs. I wondered how this terrific old man had made it through life with only half of his fingers. I was later to learn that not only had he made it through life. He had won the $50,000 Telstra Art prize, the most prestigious Aboriginal art award in the country. This man was actually able to paint with half of his fingers missing.

He made me feel very welcome. I felt like I actually belonged there. In time, I would refer to him as "Grandpa". Some years later, I would ask him for help to get young men from the east coast over to Arnhem Land to go through ceremony since much of that has been lost through assimilation. He answered, "Yes." We could go to Gan Gan for ceremony but we would need our own song since we couldn't steal one of theirs. I was so involved in the process at the time that I helped a local songwriter, Barry Cedric, write and record a song suitable for the initiation ceremony. I still have a copy in my computer waiting for the day when the stars line up.

Gawirrin, as a young man, could still remember discovering the bodies of the Yolgnu killed by a police party at the Gan Gan massacre sometime around 1911. My adopted brother, Maylia, relayed the story to me one afternoon while we were fishing.

A surveyor had gone missing in the Gan Gan area and had not returned to his base camp. Trepang fishermen were killed by Aboriginals in the Caledon Bay area of North East Arnhem Land after a number of Yolngu women were raped. In another incident on Woodah Island, two white men named Fagan and Traynor were killed. A police officer investigating the deaths, Constable Albert McColl, was subsequently also killed by Yolngu people. McColl had handcuffed a Yolngu woman as part of a plan to catch Dhakiyarr but was killed by a spear through the heart while being led by the woman to where she had told him.

Blame was doled out immediately on the Dhalwangu living at Gan Gan. The punitive party gunned down all in sight just near the sacred water hole that Barama had risen from. The only person to survive out of the whole tribe was a man called Butja Butjami. The rest of them were slaughtered. To escape, he jumped into the water hole, submerged himself under the lily pads, and stayed submerged for a good time after the gunshots had died down.

Malaluba Gumana is one of his descendants. She is a granddaughter to Butja Butjami. Malaluba won the 2013 Telstra Bark Painting Award. She resides at Gan Gan to this day. These atrocities weren't reported in the mainstream press. What is a blight on this country's history, when taken in context, is that it happened only about a decade before my father was born. That is very recent history and is not something that is talked about in terms of the history that is taught to our children in the schools.

The tragedy gets worse, if that's possible. The surveyor that had gone missing turned up a couple of days after the bloodshed. As the sole survivor, he carried all of the Dhalwangu bloodlines with him. From that one person, the bloodline over the years built up again into the current-day Dhalwangu tribe. After fishing, we both walked to the massacre site, stopped and then paid homage to those souls departed.

In 1932, five Japanese Dhakiyarr were camping. The killings triggered panic in Darwin, capital of the Northern Territory, generating fears that Aborigines who were the majority of the population in the Territory at the time, might stage an uprising. A punitive expedition was proposed by police to "teach the Blacks a lesson". In 1928, during a previous "punitive expedition" in the Northern Territory, police killed up to 110 Aboriginal men, women, and children. It was an event that was known as the Coniston Massacre.

Many feared another such slaughter. Therefore, a party from the Church Missionary Society travelled to Arnhem Land and persuaded Dhakiyarr and three other men, who were sons of a Yolngu elder, Wonggu, to return to Darwin with them for trial. In Darwin, to the horror of the missionaries, Dhakiyarr was sentenced to death by hanging, and the three other men were sentenced to twenty years of hard labour. On appeal to the High Court of Australia, Dhakiyarr's sentence was quashed, and he was released from jail. However, he disappeared. Rumors suggested that he had been killed by the police.

The resulting crisis threatened to bring about even more bloodshed. To defuse the situation, a young anthropologist, Donald Thomson, offered to investigate the causes of the conflict. He travelled to Arnhem Land on a mission that many said would be suicidal, and got to know and understand the people who lived there. After seven months of investigation, he persuaded the Federal Government to free the three men convicted of the killings. He returned with them to their own country, living for over a year with their people, documenting their culture.

He formed a strong bond with the Yolngu people. In 1941, he persuaded the Army to establish a special reconnaissance force of Yolngu men known as the Northern Territory Special Reconnaissance Unit including Wonggu and his sons to help repel Japanese raids on the northern coastline of Australia.

Wonggu (c.1880-1959), who was an Aboriginal leader, was born into the Djapu clan from Caledon Bay, North East Arnhem Land, Northern Territory. The Djapu are part of a larger group of the indigenous inhabitants of North East Arnhem Land who call themselves Yolngu (the people), and others Balanda (outsiders). In the past, non-Aborigines often but incorrectly referred to the Yolngu as the Balamumu. When Donald Thomson met him in the mid 1930s, he judged him to be over 50 years of age. By then, he was the senior elder of the Djapu with more than 40 wives and at least 60 children.

There is a similar story concerning Trepangers using Aboriginal women for their own purposes. The story is from a small fishing village called Kurramine Beach in North Queensland. The road that leads into Kurramine Beach is called Murdering Point. An almost identical story unfolded at Kurramine Beach as what happened at Calendon Bay. The story was painted on the wall of the hotel and told of the Aboriginal women being raped and Aboriginal men taking retribution on the Trepangers. The retribution on Aboriginal men, women, and children left a large number dead, another blight on Australia's dark history.

That story was painted on the wall of the Kurramine Beach Hotel Resort over a decade ago. It suddenly disappeared from the wall where it was originally painted. It was painted over by brand new owners who took part in the creation of a brand-new story. The new story was painted on a wall in a different part of the hotel. My bottom jaw dropped when I read the new sanitised version. I worked at the hotel every Saturday night for nearly five years. You can imagine how I felt to see people's lives painted over and Aboriginal people once again being made the demons. Sexual mistreatment of Aboriginal women was Australia's watered-down version for the word "rape."

In 1937-38, Wonggu and his family left the Caledon Bay area and settled at Yirrkala, a mission station on the Gove Peninsula established by the Methodists in 1935, in response to the Caledon Bay massacre. The drawing together of different groups created tensions and Wonggu's family was involved in a period of lethal conflict. He provided scouts and guides to assist Thomson's Special Reconnaissance Unit in World War II.

Wonggu, "King of the Balamumu," had caught the imagination of the popular press in the 1930s. His name was prominent in sensational reports of the incidents in Arnhem Land. Ion Idriess and Victor Hall characterised him as an evil genius in their accounts of the Caledon Bay massacre. Thomson disagreed, respecting him as a "gallant warrior, frank, and completely fearless." He described Wonggu as "a tall, powerful man with [an] intelligent face, deep set eyes, and a heavy beard."

Fred Gray remembered him as an impressive man, in whose company he spent the happiest time of his life. Wonggu died on 7 June 1959 at Yirrkala. A man of influence, authority, and charisma, he represented a romantic and little known aspect of Northern Territory history. More importantly, the events in which he was involved drew attention to the issues of Aboriginal justice and rights to land.

Back at Gan Gan, the didgeridoo no longer serenaded the night. The clapsticks had become strangely silent and community life went back to normal. Since it was the wet season and getting around was challenging, to say the least, a group of us in a four-wheel drive decided to head over to Lake Evella. It was a comedy on four wheels. It seemed that every kilometre or two that we negotiated in the wet, we become bogged down. Someone would grab an axe out of the back cover a couple saplings down, lift the back of the vehicle with the saplings and a couple would push. We must've repeated this performance five or six times for the trip eventually landing in Lake of Evella.

The focal point of attention in a small community is the community store. I was out of tobacco. The tobacco was in stock but the Eftpos machine was down and they required cash for a transaction. A newly adopted brother of mine averted an emergency and came up with the cash. It was getting towards dark, so we headed off into the great unknown and for some strange reason, we only were bogged down once on the way home. We indulged in kangaroo cooked underground in the coals this night. This was the sweetest meat of any sort I'd ever tasted. I haven't tasted anything near as good since.

The two weeks were nearly up. It was with much trepidation that I contemplated going home. Maylia would tell me "You've now been through law." That didn't make sense to me at the time since I didn't have the operation. However, in later years I would come to appreciate what he was trying to tell me. It was still too wet to drive to Nhulunbuy, so we had to get a charter plane out.

Sharon helped us financially to all get home. We said our goodbyes and flew into Nhulunbuy. We flew down the coastal strip. To this day, it has been the most spectacular plane trip that I've ever been on. This is especially true for me, who is not big on real planes in the first place. It was a good feeling taking a small part and a swag for a very first time on an airplane will. It was with much pridethat I handed over my swag to departures. Written in black felt pen was Greg Reid, Cairns. I thought to myself, if they only had half an idea of where we've been and what was seen, we could stamp out racism in the blink of an eyelid. The ceremony was over and it was back to work at radio BBM 98.7 FM.

There was a new man behind the microphone. He had a new awareness, a new understanding of the sacredness the Yolngu hold in their ceremonies and in their way of life. So much of everything that they do has a sacredness to it and which they were unbelievably willing to share. On Monday morning with a flick of a microphone switch, I was back in business.

Life in Cairns was good and I kept receiving new insights each day. I understood the power of the Mind just a little more each day. I had previously used the power of the Mind to turn around a log floating down a creek and bring it in to my feet where I stood on the bank. The path to greater awareness cures by authority and cooperation with the Holy Spirit.

Since I was also employed as Senior Broadcaster at radio BBM, I was responsible directly or indirectly for fourteen other volunteers at the radio station. I was responsible for their training and development with the help of the CEO.

For many indigenous people, *TalkBlack* was their first opportunity to be able to talk out about the issues that affected them and not have to fear any reprisal. For those who grew up on a mission, this was particularly liberating for them. Imagine having to ask the Protector if you can go to town. Or on the other hand, if you can marry.

These were new and exciting times for many indigenous people. They could call from anywhere in Australia with a free 1800 number. They could also talk about any issue that they wanted to. One caller phoned in and said, "Greg, you've got a very old soul and I can feel you from here." The difference between that call and an average every-day Australian making a call, was the word "feel." Many people "talk" but so few have the ability to feel.

Another caller that stays in my mind is a woman who plucked up the courage to phone the station and tell me about her sexual abuse as a child. She was very brave and she said to me, "Are you still there, Greg?" I answered, "Yes, I am. I'm just having a bit of trouble talking at the moment because tears are running down the cheeks of my face." I wasn't afraid to feel her pain.

At a 100 to 1 chance, I decided to enter *TalkBlack* into the 2006 Queensland Media Awards in the category of Best Coverage of Indigenous Affairs (All Media). The awards were sponsored by the Queensland Media, Entertainment and Arts Alliance.

The section I entered was open to all media. I was competing against The Australian Newspaper and one of their best journalists, Tony Koch, who had previously won four Walkleys Awards. The Walkleys Awards are recognised as the epitome in Australian journalism awards. If that didn't make the competition hard enough, the other entry I was up against was the ABC TV. BBM was a community broadcaster and we came humbly with our hat in our hand and a belief in our heart.

When the announcement was made for our section, they called out ". . . and the winner is: Greg Reid from Bumma Bippera Media in Cairns." They then played some of the audio of our submission.

We didn't go with the main media crowd to the parties that we were invited to. We just eased back and had a few quite celebratory drinks at the same venue the awards were held at. My youngest brother and middle son were able to be there with me along with the CEO and his wife, and the chairman with his wife. It took a couple of days to find my feet back on the ground and then it was back to business.

The building where we worked had a lift that went down into the car park. In the car park, there was a room to access the ventilator for the lift. I befriended a young man and his partner who were living on the street. I got to know them reasonably well over the ensuing weeks and would quite often give them a couple of toast slices with a cup of coffee. One of the other broadcasters from BBM, Auntie Evelyn, was doing the same thing, except she had invited them up into the kitchen of the offices and studio of BBM.

Unbeknown to us, the young man was holding the girl captive in the ventilator room where he was raping her and holding her against her will. Both of them were also sniffing paint. The truth began to see the light of day when the young man with a knife held at the young woman's side brought her up to the offices and studios of BBM. One of the staff alerted the CEO, who in turn alerted me and he asked me to come "off air" to help. I was in the middle of presenting *TalkBlack,* so my time frame was limited. I came out to where the young man was standing with a knife against the girl's ribs and I told him, "Get out of here! What the hell do you think you're doing?"

He took a wrong turn and went past me down the walkway to the studios. I followed him and once again yelled at him, "Get the hell out of here." For whatever reason, my voice seemed more powerful than his knife and he left the studio area. I followed him out to the foyer, where I was informed by a staff member the police were on their way. He was not able to reach the bottom of the building before.

I have seen the girl on numerous occasions since the incident. She has since been able to live a reasonable life since she had suffered some temporary brain damage from the paint. She has children and a partner. She often gives me a smile remembering full well, that it was something totally amazing the day she witnessed someone's voice having power over a knife.

It's hard to describe the impact *TalkBlack* has had on a large proportion of indigenous people across Australia. A recent comment by Florence Onus gives some perspective of the effect that *TalkBlack* has had. Florence has been a campaigner for indigenous rights all her life. She is currently an Aboriginal Advocate for Social Justice. She was also the manageress of the indigenous radio station in Townsville when *TalkBlack* was at its peak. She recently stated, "He was the best thing that ever happened to Black media in this country."

CHAPTER 6

THE QUINKANS

My spiritual life was leading me right to heaven's door. My career reached heights that I'd never imagined possible. However, my personal life had fallen into a deep dark well. The worst part was I had been in this very same place before and had not learned my lesson. They say you keep getting the same lesson over and over until you learn it. In the personal relationships department, I wasn't passing my grades. We went to relationship counselling a number of times and the counsellor was very good. In the end, we were both too stubborn to learn the lesson that was available.

The counsellor suggested that we communicate a little better by taking a pencil to our communications sessions. The idea was whoever held the pencil could talk for as long as they wanted to without their partner interrupting. When the first party finished talking, the person handed the pencil to the other one and they could commence to talk without interruption. While this sounds like a good idea in theory, in practice, I found myself struggling to talk without interruption even though I had the pencil.

On top of that, there were the normal family interruptions from the girls. That nearly always seem to coincide with the precious fifteen minutes we had put aside to be together. I tried to get those few minutes as our sacred time and not to be interrupted. However, I was fighting a lone battle.

In the middle of all this mayhem, I came around the corner of the house after lunch to go back to work and I ran into a living breathing Wandjina. He had an orange hood and a near pure white face. He stood nearly 2½ m tall and was about a metre wide. In broad daylight at 12.30 pm, I was face-to-face with a Wandjina for the first time.

I had heard a little bit about them but not too much. Later that day, I had the opportunity to get to a computer. I absorbed everything possible regarding Wandjinas. Up until that point, I couldn't find one with an orange hood. Therefore, I was lost on the reason of the visitation. It would be many years later that I would come to understand what they really were: spirit beings that have never been born and will never die. They rejoice in seeing us make our long-awaited approach, they welcome us, and they reveal their great wisdom to any sincere seekers. The day, the hour and the moment will remain etched firmly into my soul beyond this lifetime.

After three-month's of counselling, my partner and I still couldn't find common ground. We decided to part and to put the house on the market. Because it was a rushed sale, it sold for quite a bit less than we had hoped for. I temporarily took up lodging in a nearby caravan park before renting a house in a much better part of town.

The original Creation Wandjina story is told by Mabel King in Chapter 4, page of this book. The following is an expanded view of the creation story.

The land of the Wandjina is a vast area of about 200,000 square kilometres of lands, waters, sea and islands in the Kimberley region of North West Australia with continuous culture dating back at least 60,000 years. The Worora, Ngarinyin, and Wunumbal people are the three Wandjina tribes. These tribal groups are the custodians of the oldest known figurative art which is scattered throughout the Kimberley.

The Wandjina came down from the Milky Way during Dreamtime and created the Earth and all its inhabitants. Wandjina then looked upon the inhabitants, realised the enormity of the task, and returned home to bring more Wandjina. They were aided in their task by the Dreamtime snake.

Aboriginal people in the Kimberley believe the Wandjina continue to control everything that happens on the land and in the sky and sea. Today, the Aboriginal tribes of the Worora, Ngarinyin, and Wunumbal still revere the Wandjina and only certain individuals are given permission to paint them.

Dreaming tracks crisscross Australia and trace the journeys of the ancestral spirits as they created the land, animals, and lores. These dreaming tracks are sometimes called "Songlines" as they record the travels of these ancestral spirits who "sung" the land into life. These Songlines are recorded in traditional songs, stories, dance, and art. They carry significant spiritual and cultural connection to knowledge, customs, ceremony, and lore of many Aboriginal nations and Torres Strait Islander language groups.

Songlines are intricate maps of land, sea, and country. They describe travel and trade routes, the location of waterholes, and the presence of food, in many cases. Songlines on the earth are mirrored by sky songlines, which allowed people to navigate vast distances of this nation and its waters. The extensive network of song lines can vary in length from a few kilometres to hundreds of kilometres. One such songline begins in Mornington

Island in the Gulf of Carpentaria and winds its way all the way to Melbourne.

Similarly, the Seven Sisters' songline covers more than half the width of the continent, from deep in the central desert out to the west coast, while others connect the Gulf of Carpentaria with the Snowy Mountains near Canberra. Aboriginal language groups are connected through the sharing of songlines with each language group responsible for parts of the songline.

Songlines have been passed down for thousands of years and are central to the existence of Aboriginal and Torres Strait Islander people. They are imperative to the preservation of Aboriginal and Torres Strait Islander cultural practices.

For Aboriginal and Torres Strait Islander people, the Dreamtime describes a time when the Earth, people and animals were created by the ancestral spiritual beings. They created the rivers, lakes, plants, land formations, and living creatures.

Recent archaeological discoveries have confirmed the reality of some of the Dreamtime stories. For example, those that spoke of huge mammals walking the Earth were once considered fantasy. However, discoveries of animal fossils belonging to "mega fauna", including giant mammals, confirmed that these stories were accounts of real life events, passed down by generations over tens of thousands of years. Interestingly and, of course, controversially, objects have been found on geographical sites that suggest the area had been inhabited as long ago as 174,000 BC. This contradicts the theory that Aboriginals had their roots in Africa and that inhabitants travelled from Africa to Australia about 60,000 years ago. Other researchers have suggested that Homo sapiens actually originated in Australia.

World Truth TV also states that in 1982, an examination was done on mitochondrial DNA of indigenous people including twelve full blood Aboriginals and the results were in total opposition to what they assumed was fully resolved. Nevertheless, the researcher was obliged to contradict a central tenant of the paper, stating that mitochondrial DNA puts the origin of Homo sapiens much further back and indicates that the Australian Aboriginals arose 400,000 years ago.

When I was in primary school learning social studies, we were told the Aboriginal people of this land arrived here 9,000 years ago. We were taught that was fact or that further scientific research would be needed to come up with a more accurate figure. The original people here in Australia have gone from being here 9000 years in 1968 to 50,000 years in 2016. It shouldn't take too much to jump from 50,000 to 174,000 years and one more leap to 400,000 years.

Through my work, I keep up to date on news from around the world. The most significant story that I've encountered in over 25 years in the media turned up on my desk today. New DNA technology confirms Aboriginal people as the first Australians.

A new look at ancient bones with the latest DNA technology has confirmed Australian Aboriginals as the continent's first people. Researchers say the findings overturn a 2001 paper that argued the oldest known Australian human remains found near Lake Mungo in New South Wales were from an extinct lineage of modern humans that occupied the continent before Aboriginal Australians.

This claim was based on mitochondrial DNA extracted from Mungo man's 40,000-year-old fossilised remains by a team of Australian universities, led by Dr Greg Adcock. However, Professor David Lambert from Griffith University and his colleagues have used new DNA sequencing methods to reanalyse the material from the Mungo man who was found in the World Heritage listed Wilandra Lakes region in far western New South Wales. Professor Lambert said that the latest findings were published in the 7 June 2016 in proceedings of the National Academy of Sciences. He said, "The sample from the Mungo man which we retested, contained sequences from five different European people suggesting that these all represent contamination."

The common perception of indigenous Australians leading a hunter-gatherer lifestyle before European settlement is ignoring strong evidence of sophisticated farming and agriculture practices. Historians have noted there were repeated references to indigenous people building dams and wells, planting, irrigating, and harvesting seed, preserving the surplus, and storing it in houses, sheds, or secure vessels and managing the landscape.

In his book *Dark Emu*, Mr. Pascoe argues, "There was a lot more sedentary living then we were led to believe." He revisits early explorers' accounts of seeing women harvesting yams, onions, and cultivating the land. He said there was a grain harvest and the grinding of seed into flour that once was done on a wide scale. Mr. Pascoe was surprised by the reserves of grain that were stored in secure vessels and he wondered why these facts have been conveniently deleted from our history.

In the book *The Oldest Foods on Earth* by John Newton, he tells a similar tale of a very sophisticated civilisation. He noted that Aboriginal people reared and tamed possums, emus, cassowaries, and penned young pelican chicks. He noted they use fishing nets, duck traps, and terraced farming. He noted the entire country was carefully and thoroughly farmed in a manner that left the land and its bounty in balance and in abundance.

There was also the use of fish and eel traps. Tribes that lived on the Kimberley coast lived with the fish. They actually communicated with the fish and knew their names. Dolphins or sharks all had individual names. When they fished, they called them like calling a dog that had a name. The fish listened to them, since they could hear through the water.

As recalled by David Mowaljarlai in his book *Yorro Yorro*, the sea people called out the shark's name "Kanamudj" and it came to where the people were on the shore of a little island. The shark gave one of the men a lift on his back, back to the mainland. He even goes as far as to name the shark as a black tiger shark.

He also recalls a similar story of a number of dolphins giving a group of people a ride for the men who had a fire stick tucked into their hair wallet on their head. The old people were singing out, "This is me! We're swimming! Listen to us!" They were talking to the dolphins. The dolphins called out "Ch-chooo-o … cchooo-o."

I have even heard stories that where dolphins were used to herd fish and bring them in to the shore so that they were easy to spear. Dick Roughsey, in his book *Moon over the Rainbow*, explains that prior to white men coming, there were five distinct languages in every tribe. One of those languages was the animal language where all members of the tribe communicated with the animals and the birds of this land.

There are still remnants of this left today. I have witnessed two different people talk in the language of a goanna in such a way the goanna is immobilised by the sound and the hunter simply walks up and kills his prey.

In April 2016, there was an ABC News story regarding a little-known Aboriginal heritage site in South West Victoria that has moved one step closer to UNESCO World Heritage listing with the Victoria government by announcing a $5 million plan to improve visitor facilities.

The Budji Bim lava flow landscape north of Portland is home to some of the oldest known examples of fabricated aquaculture systems in the world, as well as evidence of numerous Aboriginal settlements. The Gunditjmara people built this complex system with eel traps 6,600 years ago across 3000 Ha of land, providing them with enough sustenance to settle in one place. Their descendants have managed the land for the past fifteen years and, more recently, have been working on the application for World Heritage listing.

Few non-indigenous people have ever accessed the inner spirit world of the Aboriginal people. The one person that went right to the very core and beyond and was privy to sacred knowledge and law, was a little white girl who lived in the Channel country in the early 1900s. Her name was Alice Duncan-Kemp. She was the daughter of William and Laura Duncan of Mooraberrie station. The old wise people of the Emu tribe recognised Alice as Pinningarra. Their beloved leaf spirit had returned and was reborn in the body of this small white girl child. I believe that her book *Where Strange Gods Call* is the most complete insight into Aboriginal life that's ever been written in this country or anywhere else in the world.

She was five years old when her father died in February 1907. Her brother also died at just 4½ years of age. She had one sister called Trixie. Her father had emigrated from Scotland in 1878. He spent his early years as a stockman managing properties in coastal Queensland before he came to manage property in the Channel country called Mooraberrie. He eventually bought this property in 1894, and married a girl from the Parramatta River.

She was about to encounter the outback headlong. There was no Flying Doctor and no medical aid of any kind in those days. As a result, their eldest child died in infancy. Her father died at the age of 48, when he fell from a horse. His young widow was left to carry on a big beef project that was dear to his heart.

As with many properties at this time, Laura Duncan used the services of local indigenous maids and stockmen. What was unusual about this exchange of labour was the local Eaglehawk tribe was allowed to carry on and practice their traditional beliefs in and around station work commitments. They took Alice into the tribe as if she was one of their own, and calling her Mingari. Mingari was the daughter of Earth Mother and the Moon God. Members of the Eaglehawk tribe were given beef from cattle raised on the property, flour, sugar, and tea. The Eaglehawks were still able to fill most of their dietary requirements with local bush tucker. Most importantly, they could still practise their ceremonies. Work on the cattle property revolved around tribal practices. This was one of very few places in all of Australia where this occurred.

The history starts with the sacred sword shaped, 5 ft long God stick encrusted with carved symbols. It is a sacred relic which, to the initiated, gave the history of the tribe since its inception, and which was the voice of Bahloo the moon tribe and the Earth Mother.

Many people know that Moses was given two stone tablets, and that the commandments were written in God's own hand. It is quite possible that 50,000 years before Moses received his two stone tablets, in the Channel country in Australia two long flat stones 20 inches long and 2-4 inches wide called the Oolbris stones were known to exist in the Eaglehawk tribe. These stones were sung by medicine men and law men. Each stone had a series of symbols engraved on the sides and in the middle.

There is no easy way to describe the meaning of "sung by a medicine man or law man." Only a Master, medicine man or lawman has the capabilities of such a feat. The easiest explanation would be to say that the medicine man puts some of his Mind in the stone. These sacred stones carved in the law, existed quite possibly 40,000 years before Moses received his stone tablets. What makes this even more amazing is that this is a group of people we were told couldn't read or write.

The Aboriginal man who was Alice's mentor as she grew up, was given the name Moses. He cared for her just as her father would have. As Alice and Moses were riding out to some backcountry, a storm came up and they were forced to seek shelter in a sacred place they shouldn't have been in. Inside the shelter, was an elder who was the Guardian of a shining stone symbol that was the god or spirit of the Wundjina country.

This stone was 24 inches long, a foot in width and weighed about 30 pounds. Alice, because of her status within the Eaglehawk tribe, was privileged to see this Holy of Holies, Moonka Karanya, the Lizard God of the Mulligan River tribes.

It was a timeless, living symbol of life and power to an ancient people. The elder that she had a shelter, Old Cunjer stroked the rock with his long narrow fingers and caused it to talk in short chittering chirps. By slanting the stone to catch the West wind, he then caused the stone to speak in shrill coughing calls that echoed across the flats. If Old Cunjer stroked the smooth surface of the stone lightly with the palm of his hand, he could make it roar and bellow like an angry bull.

Alice Duncan Kemp was privy to see all of these amazing sacred objects simply because she was reincarnated as Mingari. Alice saw many sacred objects that even fully initiated men in the tribe were not able to cast their eyes on. One particular stone, the "Ooltharu" or "history stone", had deeply scored crisscrossed markings in the shapes of Vs, diamonds and half diamonds. All of the abstract drawings reminded Alice of Euclid, who is quite often referred to as the father of mathematics.

Alice was privy to visit many places first-hand, including sites that revealed grey-white slabs of rock etched and engraved with sacred and secret hieroglyphs. These were the home of the Dhoorabas, stone altars of the Aborigines and often with these relics were found pointed 10 bars. They were cylindrical stones about 10 to 12 inches in height. These curious looking off-white stones with rounded or flat bases were called ritual "womma guru" meaning the heart of the snake. Womma is the name for the cream-coloured sandhill carpet snake, the Aboriginal symbol of getting food and the assimilation of wisdom.

There have been several prominent archaeologistswho have made similar statements that man originated out in Australia but they were silenced by the maddening crowd that clutch onto the familiar, flat-Earth people.

In today's news, as I write this book, I came across an article about a remarkable woman from the Kimberley. Her name is Loogkoonan and she only started painting at the age of 95. She is now 105. She has her work exhibited in the Australian Embassy in Washington DC. She paints the ground as she sees it as an eagle. It immediately reminds me of a cave site that I visited near Chillagoe. As explained to me, the markings on the roof of the cave were identical to the physical features of the land immediately in front of the cave, like a topographical map.

The person explaining the cave markings had spent a number of years in the Army. He said that the only way the artists could have achieved such accuracy in the depiction of the geographical marks on the cave roof was to have been elevated to the height of a light aircraft and been able to fly safely without getting too close to the ground. The other explanation could be that the artists had an out-of-body experience, saw the ground from a great height and marked what he or she saw on the cave roof.

The Magic men and women had very specific roles. They were known by names like Clevermen, Banman, Gulka, Kadaitcha Man, and Featherfoot. Some were healers and others were sorcerers. The healers could put their hand inside someone who was ill and pull out a stingray barb, a handful of blood or lumps of fat. Each man or woman had a special way of healing. They might prescribe some bush medicine. However, sometimes there was nothing they could do because that person's time had come.

Many could dematerialise the body and create a second body many miles away. There have been numerous accounts of an individual seeing someone they know, and driving 100 km down the road only to see the same person at their destination. These men and women were masters of materialisation. The were able to materialise mind vitality into any gross material thing. They could materialise a crocodile or any living or innate thing. I have actually witnessed this amazing feat on a number of occasions.

Aboriginal people lived under a very strict law system. If anybody transgressed the law in a major way, the Kadaitcha Man was called in by the elders to point the "bone" at the transgressor. Within days, he or she was dead. That is the power of the mind. No poisons were used. It was simply that the transgressor's days were numbered, they accepted the fact and passed over.

Aboriginal people had formed one of the most technologically advanced societies in the world when white man first arrived on Australian shores. Things like the boomerang to most people is just a simple piece of wood but the angled shape with asymmetrical curves makes use of the most complicated principles of aerodynamic asymmetrical lift.

Aboriginal people made a powerful thermoplastic resin out of porcupine grass and grass tree. They beat the resin out of the grass, then cleaned it and heated it over the fire to create a sticky black substance. The resulting resin hardened as it cooled and was strong enough to bind rock to wood. This resin was used to create tools such as spears, woomeras, and axes.

They also demonstrated that they had a unique understanding of engineering, physics, and aquaculture in the design of elaborate stone fish traps in New South Wales and in Victoria at Lake Condah. They invented a type of fridge that would allow them to carry water in special bags made of wallaby skins that used the same principles of heat transfer to keep the water cool.

In addition, the didgeridoo is thought to be the world's oldest wind instrument. While it is deceptively simple in design, it is, in fact, a complicated instrument, starting from a termite hollowed small tree.

Aboriginal people invented many ways to extract food and bush medicine from Australia's landscape. They fished, hunted, rendered poisonous seeds edible, turned certain moths and grubs into delicious meals, made sweet drinks from honey and nectar and ground grass seeds to bake an early form of damper. They used tannins to treat inflammation and alkaloids to relieve pain. They extracted antiseptics, such as tea tree oil, to cure infections. Finally, they harvested latex to treat ulcers and skin conditions.

What is not commonly known are the very large numbers of Aboriginal men, women and children who were massacred in this country. It has always been conveniently overlooked by non-indigenous people and the numbers have always been kept very small.

In researching this book, I spent many hours searching many different sources for what I considered to be a number closer to the truth. That number is 2,450. It's much more likely to be three times more Aborigines who died by the bullet, poisoned, or were struck by a blow to the head from a stirrup iron removed from the saddle in pursuit of the quarry. Many of these massacres were extremely cowardly. By any standard in warfare, women and children are generally spared the bomb and the bullet.

The tribe that I was adopted into was all but exterminated. However, the records of the deaths don't appear in any of the lists of the massacres that occurred in this country. Many fit into the same category. Where I lived in Innisfail, there is current history of a similar massacre in the South Johnstone River. However, the number of these tragedies is not reflected in the figures of the massacres.

Set against a background of what some would call genocide, the chief protector of Aborigines in Western Australia from 1915 to 1936 was A. O. Neville. His thinking was mirrored throughout Australia at the time and his words still reverberate to this day. He said, "It is my belief that the assimilation of Aboriginal people of mixed descent could only occur through breeding out of the colour." This thinking came to prominence on the world stage later in the century with Nazi Germany's superior "White Aryan Race."

Aborigines' secret to survival has been their ability to adapt and change in response to the environment. We now know they have lived here at least 50,000 years and maybe even 174,000 years.

The time has arrived when the sacred is being shared by different cultures among those who seek. The real power of the Mind has already been unlocked but it was shared by only a few. Those who truly seek for the right reasons, now have access to the secrets that have been locked up for tens of thousands of years. We're beginning the age of enlightenment and many are waking.

We no longer need to turn lead to gold even though it's physically possible. The real gold lies within our hearts and those who are awakened will now shine a light for those who come behind. We as a society will go through much change and what we once thought was valuable will now be re-assessed. A small country called Bhutan is leading the way by how they measure their wealth with a yardstick called GNH, which stands for gross national happiness.

I was with my partner four years, During this time, I learned many things about the Norwegian culture. Even though the breakup was not easy, visions kept coming my way. I settled into my new abode. Within two weeks, I found myself in the middle of another vision. In this one, I saw a Wedge Tail Eagle fly right up into the deepest blue of the sky. He kept flying, higher and higher until he flew so high that he completely disintegrated. All that was left were his feathers. Anyone who picked one up would become a healer. I picked up a big tail feather.

According to the animal medicine of the Native Americans, "It is that which improves one's connection to the Great Mystery and to all Life. It includes the healing of body, mind, and of spirit. This medicine is also anything that brings personal power, strength, and understanding. It is the constant living of life in a way that brings healing to Mother Earth and to all of our associates, friends, and fellow creatures."

"Our fellow creatures, the animals, exhibit habit patterns that will relay these messages of healing to anyone astute enough to observe their lessons on how to live. The precious gifts of true medicine are free. The power lies in the wisdom and understanding of one's role in the Great Mystery, and in honouring every living thing as a teacher."

"Eagle medicine is the power of the Great Spirit, the connection to the Divine. It is the ability to live in the realm of spirit, and yet remain connected and balanced with the realm of Earth. Eagle represents a state of grace achieved through hard work, understanding, and a completion of the tests of initiation that rest in the taking of one's personal power. It is only through the trial of experiencing the lows in life as well as the highs, and through the trial of trusting one's connection to the Great Spirit, that the right to use the essence of Eagle medicine is earned."

"Eagle reminds you to take heart and gather your courage, for the universe is presenting you with an opportunity to soar above the mundane levels of life. The power of recognising this opportunity may come in the form of a spiritual test. In being astute, you may recognise the places within your soul, personality, emotions, or psyche that need bolstering or refinement. By looking at the overall tapestry, Eagle teaches you to broaden your sense of self beyond the horizon of what is presently visible. The wings of your soul will be supported by the ever-present breezes which are the breath of the Great Spirit." Taken from Medicine Cards, by Four Winds, Jamie Sam & David Carson

I fondly remember riding a horse when I was eight years old. While I was riding, a big Wedge Tail Eagle hovered above me. I remember leaving my horse and spiritually connecting with the eagle. I was uncertain of what kind of reaction I would get if I told anybody, so for the first of many times, I kept my mouth shut. Later in life, I experienced another examatosis where I turned into a beautiful woman and I'm given a choice as to which road I will go. The first choice is to stay as a beautiful woman. The second choice is to turn into an eagle. Without a moment's hesitation, I chose to become an eagle.

In Australia, the Wedge Tail Eagle is a protected species. If you want to have a feather from this bird, it's necessary to have a permit from the Department of Natural Resources. I have a tail feather that I keep in my car under the sun visor. They are especially good in clearing away negative energy from the aura or as some call it etheric double. The tribes from South America use a tail feather from the condor for the same purpose.

I've been to a number of healers. With each of them, a unique experience came as I totally gave myself to the spirit. Some use different methods. However, I found that in the end, it all pretty well works out the same. I was able to access the astral realm while they go about their work. Some healers were so advanced that they were able to see my guardian angel standing at the top of the massage table watching over me.

I moved into a new lodging in the suburb of Earlville that was given to me free of charge by a beautiful Aboriginal woman. She had heard of the predicament of my recent breakup and was happy to oblige and help in any way that she could. She was one of the stolen generations and grew up in a girls' home in New South Wales. She told me countless stories of her culture and of the little hairy men (Aboriginal spirit beings) and where I could see them. She was also 100% sure that I was of Aboriginal descent. I must've known her for over 10 years and she still maintained my Aboriginality right up until the last time I saw her.

In my lifetime, there must have been nearly 100 people who have said the same thing. Some people have done tests on my fingers, others had just said it to my face straight out. I've never used my Aboriginal name "Dharayara", so it would seem like I was Aboriginal. However, many say they can hear it in my voice. One of the joys of working at radio BBM was that every two years there was a dance and cultural festival at a place called Laura up in the Cape York Peninsula, in Quinkan country. For three days, different tribal groups from all over Cape York Peninsula and the Gulf descended upon an ancient Bora Ground to dance just as their ancestors did. It is a legacy going back 50,000 years or possibly 100,000 years, maybe even more.

The camping ground is situated on the beautiful Laura River that is known to have been home to the odd crocodile or two but no one seemed to care. Radio BBM would broadcast over the three days. During this time, up to 15,000 people would descend on the Laura campground. Many people would barely have enough money to cover the price of the fuel to get there and home again. Nevertheless, just like a homing pigeon, every two years community upon community would return.

Children as young as two would take centre stage, having been tutored for months before the event. Each dance would have a story that would be told during the dance. It would be done with a combination of dance movement and sometimes language. The old people would have overseen the young ones in their training for the big event, making sure that the timing was perfect. In my opinion, a really good performance is as good as any live performance in the world, be it ballroom dancing or ballet.

At one particular performance, I was yarning away with a dance leader from a community called Wooorabinda. It's an Aboriginal community that is not very far from the small town where I grew up called Comet. As I was chatting away, I asked him, "Can you smell-lemon scented gum?" He agreed he could and I said, "Well, that's awful strange because there was no-lemon scented gum that grows around here." The only place I can remember lemon-scented gum was when I was riding from the back dam to the Bora Ground on Nine Mile.

I saw the same man later in the day. He advised me that one of their most dear and revered elders had passed away the previous night. We both agreed the country was calling us before her passing. Only a month ago, I ordered some bush tucker (food from the Australian wilderness) from an online firm and in the package there was a small-lemon scented gum leaf in the order for free. I hadn't seen one for 50 years.

One of my jobs was to interview one of the Traditional Owners who, as long as I can remember, has been called an institution. I didn't have a list of questions ready. There was just me and the recorder. I sat down next to him and he asked what we were gonna talk about. At that point, he started laughing. I followed suit and we kept laughing for a full five minutes. That was the interview: five minutes of laughter. We connected at such a high level that there was no need for words. I've never done another interview like it again in my life but I sure do look forward to the day it does happen.

I was very mindful that I was in Quinkan country. It was known that there were two groups of Quinkans: the Imjim and the Timara. The Imjim were small fat-bellied bad fellows, with large ugly heads, long teeth and claws. They stole children and took them to their cave in the great red mountain. The Imjim had long knobbly tails that they used like a kangaroo to travel in giant leaps across the land. Timara was the name of the other Quinkans. They were humorous, whimsical spirits who liked to play tricks on people. However, they didn't like the Imjim stealing children and always tried to stop them.

Turramulli, the giant Quinkan, was turned into a children's book by Dick Roughsey and Percy Treseize. That was one of at least six that were turned into children's books.

While I was broadcasting at the Laura dance and cultural festival, I came down with a really bad dose of the flu. It was so bad that I had to go to bed and wasn't able to fulfill my duties behind the microphone. I was in bed for two days. In those two days, I was visited by the Imjim Quinkan who danced all over my chest. I said, "Take me" but, quite obviously, my time had not yet come. I did recover to full health with yet another experience from the indigenous spirit world firmly etched in my mind. Maybe that's what Tommy George was laughing about. He could see Imjim jumping all over me.

The Laura Dance and Cultural Festival is the largest of its kind in Australia. It attracts a wide variety of people, from all backgrounds and nationalities. It had for many years, attracted an alternate crowd that was left over from the hippie movement. They came and erected Wig Wam tents, banged on their bongo drums into the night, and several of the young women would bathe bare breasted in the Laura River. How do I know such a thing? I went down, swam in the river, and ended up in conversation with a couple of them trying to understand what the drawcard was in such a remote part of Australia.

Their attraction was the indigenous culture and the sharing and caring that went with it. They had opted out of mainstream Western society and travelled to various folk festivals and indigenous cultural festivals across the country. I was never able to determine how they managed the financial side of so much travelling. I did invite one lady to do an interview on the radio the following morning. She turned up just as she had promised. Right in front of my manager, she walked up, wrapped her arms around me, hugged me, and said, "You've got wonderful karma." It was such a positive start to the broadcast and things were only getting better.

We finished our last broadcast for the day. We packed up our gear and started off down the dusty road again, vowing to be back in two years' time.

Back in Cairns, it took some re-adjusting to city life even though we had only been away for five days. While doing my radio program *TalkBlack,* I could sense uneasiness among many of the listeners. We started discussing a grassroots organisation that would reflect the real aims and ambitions of indigenous people. I organised a march and rally in Cairns and a couple of hundred grassroots people turned up.

We had a police escort because I don't think they trusted us. We engaged and encouraged grassroots speakers to take the stand and share their viewpoint of their life and their struggle. A number of very engaging speakers spoke that day. We then encouraged a similar event to take place in Townsville, which took place about three weeks later.

Among all this unrest, a man on Palm Island called Mulrunji Doomadgee was walking around the island when he saw a police wagon go past and he yelled out, "Who let the dogs out?" The police taking offence to this, arrested him and tried to put him in the watch house on Palm Island. At the doorway of the watch house, an altercation broke out between him and the arresting officer.

What happened after that we may never know completely but, what is for sure, Mulrunji Doomadgee died after being incarcerated in Palm Island. The coroner found that the police left and didn't go to his assistance, despite cries for help. They later made no attempt to resuscitate him. This arrest was the spark that lit the fire of the riots that ultimately burned down the police house on Palm Island. Some of the people responsible were arrested, but the worst was yet to come. This was 147th death of an Aboriginal person in custody in the year of 2004.

Within two days, my manager asked if I would like to go to Palm Island to help calm the tensions. I jumped at the chance. In 24 hours I was doing my radio program from 4K1G in Townsville. The next day I travelled to Palm Island where I broadcast live from the island. Lex Wotton was convicted of inciting the Palm Island riot.

Mr Wotton was later convicted of inciting a riot and served 19 months in jail before being released on parole.

Stewart Levitt of Levitt Robinson continues to represent the Palm Island community in their battle for justice with a Palm Island Residents Racial Discrimination class action that the company has instigated. They also offered their services pro bono to represent the riot leader, Lex Wotton. Stewart Levitt, featured on the SBS's *Living Black*, programed a detailed account of the tragic events that occurred on Palm Island in 2004. The differential treatment of an Indigenous Community, so recent in our Australian history, is a harrowing story and one Levitt Robinson is passionate about revealing to ensure equality before the law. For the Island community, it is about being recognised and treated as equal so that the next generation of Indigenous children can live in the safe environment that every parent wants for their child, rather than in fear of guns and alien power.

The events of Palm Island even further galvanised the grassroots movement that was growing and fueled even further by the riots on Palm Island. A friend and I travelled to Townsville to meet up with the principal of Levitt Robertson Solicitors, Stewart Levitt. A large group of us then went out for dinner to a restaurant in Townsville.

Townsville and many other towns in the North were responsible for what is known as "Blackbirding." Blackbirding is the coercion of people through trickery and kidnapping to work as labourers. In the 1870s, the blackbirding trade focused on supplying labourers to plantations, particularly the sugar cane plantations of Queensland. The first documented practice of a major blackbirding industry for sugar cane labourers occurred between 1842 and 1904. Those blackbirded were recruited from the indigenous populations of nearby Pacific islands or Northern Queensland. In the early days of the pearling industry in Western Australia at Nickol Bay and Broome, local Aborigines were blackbirded from the surrounding areas.

The taxi driver pointed out to me one evening, the exact place where a building stood in the late 1800s where it was possible to go in and buy a slave or half a dozen. This was in Cairns in Spence Street where slavery was accepted by those who owned the plantations and the businesses that were happy to do business with the plantation owners.

There will come a time when Australia's history will need to be rewritten and the stories of slavery and massacres and stolen generations can be told. Many in the field estimate that over 2000 Aboriginal people were slaughtered for no obvious reason other than someone wanted to steal their land.

The installation of a statue has re-opened deep wounds in the state's North. The memorial to Robert Towns, the founder of Townsville, has outraged South Sea Islanders who say he started the Queensland slave trade. More than 55,000 people, mostly men, were brought from Vanuatu in the Solomon's and 80 surrounding islands, under what Australia called the indentured labour trade. This is another name for slavery. In Townsville, Mackay, Cairns, and many other small towns in between slavery had become normalised.

Non-indigenous children from this period were quite often educated to think that a man of colour was a lesser being. Many Australians were taught this and, in turn, they taught their children that Aboriginal people were of lower intellect. As a nation, we only saw what we wanted to see and through my journey, I have seen a very different picture.

People like Stewart Levitt of Levitt Robinson, who give of their time pro bono to help indigenous people regain their dignity, are a godsend. I had three more trips to Townsville and on one such trip, I met a woman who, in time, became my second wife. She was steeped in her culture. We spent many hours discussing ways of forming a treaty and getting young boys back to their culture by going through the initiation ceremony again. She had four children and lived in Yarrabah.

Life continued at radio BBM and, at this point, we were reaching out to 53 other communities across Australia including Melbourne and Darwin. Each community would receive the signal via a decoder box that needed to be set on a specific channel to receive the broadcast. By this time, *TalkBlack* had become an institution in many households. One elderly lady showed me the clock on the wall and explained that when it's 5 to 9 AM, that's when I get my coffee and sat in this chair. Everything had to be all done by 9 o'clock, including all the housework, so that she could sit down and listen to *TalkBlack*.

While the program was doing fantastically well, the actual radio station was in trouble. As an organisation, much of our reporting to our funding body, the Australian government, had fallen into disarray. As a result, superannuation wasn't being paid, tax wasn't being paid to the tax office, and many other anomalies weighed heavy on our future. That was just the tip of the iceberg. Since nobody will benefit from going any further, I'll leave the rest of the problems submerged like the main part of the iceberg.

My second wife and I were married in a registry office in Cairns. We were later given a beautiful gift of a traditional wedding in Yarrabah. We were told that it was the first traditional wedding held there in 50 years. For first part of the ceremony, we travelled by boat with the bride's father to a special place where we were immersed naked in a sacred water hole. Prior to this, the bride's father hit the water with branches from a tree to awaken the ancestral spirits so they would bless us. Upon embarking from the water hole, we were not allowed to dry ourselves with a towel. We had to let the sun dry us naturally. I still hold this part of the ceremony very special in my heart. I have much gratitude for the bride's father who guided us through this process.

On our way to where we were going to spend the night, we went to cross the creek. When I went to put my foot on the brake pedal, it just went to the floor. My partner was yelling out, "Brakes, brakes!" We got to the creek with some speed and crossed it in one piece. I got out on the other side to check the brake fluid container under the bonnet. There wasn't a drop of brake fluid in it. We proceeded on cautiously and made it to our destination without any further trouble. Three days later, we drove cautiously into Yarrabah, bought some brake fluid and filled up the container.

It never leaked another drop after that. However, we had come from Cairns and crossed the Yarrabah Range where a brake failure could have led to death in the blink of an eyelid. I drove the car three more years and never again leaked any more brake fluid.

On Saturday afternoon, the actual wedding was held at one of the beaches. Traditional practices that had not been enacted for 50 years were once again part of a marriage ceremony. The elders were really happy to see some of the traditional practices coming back. We were happy to be part of that process. The food was all home-cooked and given with love. This reminds me that I was talking to an elderly gentleman who explained to me he had just had his good pocketknife stolen. It just so happened the brand was a Henry Boker. That was the exact brand I had in my pocketknife pouch on my belt. Without a moment's hesitation, I pulled it out and handed it to the old man. A local musician, who was a friend of ours, provided us with the music and for all intents and purposes, we could have been in Hawaii.

The event finished reasonably early and we headed off to a beach shack about 12km from where the actual wedding was held. There was no electricity or running water but the surroundings were beauty personified. This land had been kept intact for the last 100,000 years and it still held plenty of secrets.

On our second day at our beach retreat, I decided to go for a late afternoon walk. I could feel a presence in the camp, yet there were no vehicles and no obvious signs of human activity. I walked and walked a good distance past some dilapidated bush shacks and still couldn't find any signs of human presence. I turned around and walked back to our camp, where I'd come from. On the way back, on the right-hand side sitting in one of the shacks, was an old man about 200 years old with silver hair right down to the floor boards of the humpy.

I yelled out, "Hey old man, did they leave you behind?" In the blink of an eyelid, the old man turned into a massive red dog. This dog would have been 10 m tall. He was massive. I instantly recognised that he was a spirit dog and I started to talk to him. I said, "Hey, it's me, Greg. You know me." At that point, I didn't know if the dog knew me or not. What I did know is that I couldn't outrun a spirit dog. I was trembling inside but I didn't want to let the dog know I was afraid. I, therefore, walked carefully very consciously back to the camp where I told my wife about the events of the last 20 minutes. She replied, "That's the Red Dog. He guards this country."

The following day, I told her father the same story and I received the same answer, "That's the Red Dog; he guards this country." I think that's about the most scared I've ever been, the day that I encountered the red dog in Yarrabah. I would find out ten years later that the old man I saw appears before someone that is a healer. He manifests himself on the Earth plane when the healer has reached a new level of proficiency, with his healing capacity having been greatly enriched.

There were many stories in Yarrabah. Some were mystery, some were history and, of course most were factual. One of the myths was about a road that was blocked on the way to a sacred beach. Everyone we asked, told us the same story. It was blocked at the top. We had just bathed in the sacred water hole only days before. I felt the spirit was within me. I decided to take the car, a Falcon station wagon, where not even a four-wheel-drive had dared to go. The tracks on the road were gouged out at least a foot. Most of the way it was a foot wide so there were only two tiny pieces where the tyres could drive on. One slip-up and the car would be sitting on its belly with no traction for the tyres,. This is called "dry bogged".

I planted my foot on the accelerator at the bottom and jammed it down real hard. It was like I was on the horse in the Man from Snowy River. If I slackened off speed or veered slightly off the track, we were history. Never before in my life, had I driven a car like I did that day. I was a man on a mission. I drove it to the very top, only to find that the road is not blocked at all. On the top was a caravan with various gear around it.

The caravan looked like an outpost guarding something. I walked over to the van, picked up a steel crowbar, went over to a cleared area and drove it hard into the ground saying aloud (to no one listening), "One day the law will be brought back to this land." It all happened in an instant but the words, the intent and what is written will be.

We drove back down the perilous track without speaking a word. However, since I was feeling in such good form that day, we stopped to make friends with some wild horses at the bottom of the track. I can't really explain what was upon me that day but this brumby stallion knew me and I befriended him out on the flat country.

He allowed me to run my hand all over him. My wife was able to explain which groups of horses were the wild ones and which were the town horses. At that point, Yarrabah was overrun by Yarraman. There was a palomino stallion that had townsfolk frightened if he chased a mare in heat through the streets. Anyway, that day I approached the second brumby stallion and the result was the same. He didn't run away or take off. He allowed me to go up to talk to him.

It was a day like I've never ever had before. I certainly look forward to having another one again. To the people of Yarrabah, "thank you. You treated me like one of your own." The holiday was over way too soon, as most holidays are. I had to return to work. I haven't told too many people about the story of the red dog until this book. However, I would not urge anyone to go looking for him. He is more than likely will go looking for you.

As a family, we spent a number of camping trips back at this same beach. The children loved it too, apart from collecting firewood which they didn't think was in their department. One night we went for a walk along the beach and as we walked, the shadows of six other people made their appearance in front of us. No one was game to look around; we just walked knowing that there was a presence. In the end, just to prove I wasn't seeing thing,s I said, "Let's turn around and go back the other way."

We turned around and went in the opposite direction. The shadows of six people were out in front of us again. By this time, we all knew what was happening. The children were quite scared. I said to the kids, "Just walk slowly, take one step at a time, and look at the light where the camp is."

By the time we got near the camp, the kids just ran off towards the light to see their mum. She explained that they were the "old people" who had passed over and were guarding and watching over us. They were the spirit people.

CHAPTER 7

THE WISE OLD WOMAN

My job situation was deteriorating daily as the organisation went closer to financial ruin and my second marriage was coming apart at the seams.

My marriage ended. I moved out of the family home, packed up my camping gear, and headed off into the great unknown. As Senior Broadcaster, I was given the use of a grey Falcon station wagon as part of my salary package. With the back seat folded forward, it made an excellent place to sleep on a piece of foam. Since I didn't want my now ex-wife finding where I was, I made camp on an isolated place on the Mulgrave River. It was a remote campsite with no showers or toilets. I used to bathe in the river each morning in the cold and again at night. The river didn't get any warmer in between the two times I took to taking my bath.

I would boil water in my billy for hot water to aid in shaving. I used the side, rear view mirror of the car so I could see where the razor was going. I had a fire each night and bit by bit found a way to put myself back together again. It was all very simple, fresh water from the Mulgrave River, plenty of firewood, a small barbecue, and an esky (a cooler). I cleaned my clothes at the laundromat in Gordonvale, where one day I met my ex-wife's father and auntie. The auntie offered me a cabin to stay in at Back Beach Yarrabah and my ex's father offered me money.

I thanked them for their kindness and consideration, then went on my way. I stayed out on the Mulgrave River site for approximately two months. Every morning I would drive into Cairns to do my radio program. Not one person on all of planet Earth knew where I was camped. That's just the way I wanted it. After two months had gone by, I weighed up my options. I figured that I was ready for life back in town. I booked into a caravan park called Cool Waters.

I was still in camp mode, sleeping in the back of the car at night. However, in this camp, I had progressed to a fridge/freezer-style esky. I also erected a tent in which to put my other belongings. This was to be one of the most amazing times of my life, even though I didn't understand it all at the time.

As I drove into my campsite, I couldn't but help notice small white pyramid markers on each side of the road. From the massive one at Garradunga in the shape of a house to these small markers, the trail of synchronicity I was following was starting to make sense. There was also the white triangle on the side of the mountain near where I was living, that sometimes looked like a massive pyramid. I was really starting to feel at home.

I'd only been at the caravan park three days, when I started to have trouble sleeping. I encountered the Wandjina spirit beings-archangels entering my body into my chest night after night. It got to a point where I could no longer sleep. I would get up and walk the dimly-lit streets, kilometre after kilometre. Somewhat tired out, I would go back to bed and the process would start all over again. The Wandjina would return.

The only comfort I had were the words of David Mowaljarlai, author of *Yorro Yorro,* who said to me previously, "The Wandjina have come to you." At this time, I also recall some words he mentioned on the telephone and now they seemed to be having meaning in my life, "You are an awakened one." I was truly beginning to feel fully awakened. This awakening process unfolded over a period of six weeks. At this point, I felt that I had authorisation to paint some of the Wandjina that I'd seen, even though I'd never painted a single image before in my life.

I also used to bathe in the creek below where I was camped against the instructions of the managers. They had a large tourist clientele who fed the freshwater turtles with bread. They didn't want any humans scaring off the turtles. Anyway, I went about my business with the stealth of an army commando and nearly every afternoon after work, I would go for a dip in the creek.

I noticed from the very first time I bathed in the creek that upon exiting and walking up a set of concrete stairs that was set on a very sharp incline, I had a distinct feeling that I felt lighter. To test my theory, I would run up the steps two or three times and not be out of breath. Every time, I felt like I had no weight or very little weight.

To test my theory even more, I invited a friend over.

I told him what had been happening with the Wandjina and the theory I had regarding the specific creek that I was bathing in every afternoon. I also mentioned the subsequent weightlessness that came after a swim. He joined me and I asked if he had ever been baptised in a creek before? He said, "No, only in a church." I then inquired if he would like to be baptised in a creek and he answered, "Yes." Subsequently, I put his head under with my right hand as I felt the spirit stream through my body and at the same time flow through my right arm and down into Damon. It was so powerful that I felt like the water was going to bubble all around us.

Since I have not been a frequent churchgoer, I was unaware of the correct procedure. He felt a presence and felt that his body was half as light as I suggested it was going to be. He decided to test the theory by running up the steep stairway. He walked back down, then turned around and ran back up to the top with literally no effort at all. I wanted to try one more person to test out this weightlessness theory. He now fully understood what I had been talking about, as I explained his body had been semi-dematerialised.

I wanted to test this theory out on someone else. Sure enough, an acquaintance in his 70s appeared on the scene. He was eager to try out this idea of dematerialisation that I had explained to him. We did everything exactly the same, although John didn't feel the need for a baptism.

He came down into the creek and I immersed him in the water just like Damon. He got out and ran up the concrete stairway with ease. He was so ecstatic that he walked back down the cement stairway and ran up to the top again. He ran as if he had no weight. He was keen to do a third time but I suggested not overdoing a good thing.

I've never felt the need to baptise anybody again and, in hindsight, the only reason I baptised Damon that particular day, is that the spirit came over me. I've not returned to that particular spot ever again, although I do bathe higher up that same creek. Occasionally, I bathe on weekends, even in winter, and I swim with the Rainbow Serpent (a water python that lives in freshwater creeks).

I was sleeping in a car with a makeshift tent and I had archangels entering my body almost every night. I was getting by on two or three hours sleep each night. Each morning, I would turn up to work and present *the TalkBlack* radio program. I would then continue to help run a radio station with 14 volunteers, a CEO, myself, and a part-time paid bookkeeper.

I had a friend who was fond of a drink or two. He would sometimes become aggressive, the more he drank. One night, he got uptight about something and he asked me outside for a fight. I agreed to go. I suggested that we walk a little bit down the road. As we did, I put my mind into his legs and made them go to jelly from wanting to fight. He got a fright and said, "Brother, I gotta sit down." He sat down and within a few minutes, he apologised for his behaviour. He then went on to explain that something strange had happened to him and his legs had turned to jelly. That was the first occasion.

On the second occasion, the same man turned up at my unit with a friend at around 2 AM in the morning. They were looking for a place to stay for the night. It was obvious that he'd been drinking again and wouldn't keep quiet and go to sleep. I yelled out a few times for him to shut up, since I had to go to work the next morning. Since this line of attack was going nowhere, I got up and told him that they both had to leave as I had work commitments the next day. My friend took offence at this and mumbled incoherently that he wanted to fight me. As he was getting up from the floor, I used my mind as I had done previously. I took his arms and legs out from under him and he fell back to the floor. I was quite upset with myself at this stage, since my valuable sleep was slipping away and my drunken friend was now lying incoherently on the floor.

I reiterated once again that he and his friend had to leave. I said that with a very forceful voice. The two of them went out the door and slipped away into the night. He has remained my friend even though he tested the boundaries of that friendship to near the breaking point. I believe that the use of the mind like this is a very sacred thing. I rarely ever use it in this way unless it can be beneficial to someone or in the case of my friend used in self-protection.

Time and time again, I hear Christ's words, "All these things you shall do and more." While the spiritual emergence was taking place, matters in my workplace were heading into a horrible headwind that threatened to become a tropical cyclone. As an organisation, we were close to bankruptcy, the superannuation had not been paid for a number of years, the tax hadn't been paid, and we were barely paying the rent.

We also had to report to our funding body, that was the Australian government, on a regular basis. We were behind in this specific area by over twelve months. Nearly every facet of the organisation's operation was dogged by sheer negligence.

Sensing the situation, the government brought in an administrator to sort the mess out. To add a little more confusion to an already out-of-control situation, our landlords told us they were not going to renew our lease and we had to move. The administrator came in wielding a samurai sword and the first person to go was the CEO. The administrator was mercenary in his approach. The power that he thought he wielded, fueled his ego that longed to be stroked daily.

He approached me and asked if I would take on the job as Project Manager to find a suitable new location for the radio station and to help oversee the building of new studios. I agreed and within four weeks, I'd found a suitable building and we engaged a builder and broadcast engineer to build a new radio station from the ground up.

Every day, however, we were reminded that BBM could fold at any time. We lived with the noose hanging over our heads on a daily basis. The studios were built within the required timeframe and we commenced broadcasting. The administrator had intimated that he was going to hire me as Manager. In fact, he played a little game between a female staff member and me. She had a better background in finance and he ultimately gave the job to her. My "reward" was that he moved me from a full-time paid position into a part-time paid position. I took objection to the demotion and resigned after ten years at BBM. Luckily, I was paid out my long service leave in proportion to the number of years I had worked there. However, in the meantime, my radio career was over.

With no immediate prospects for another job, I slowly started a downward slide into depression. It actually had its beginnings in the twelve months of uncertainty with the administrator at BBM. I went to see a psychologist about it. His opinion was that I was doing everything possible to get on top of it. He recommended that I keep on the track I was on. He didn't prescribe any antidepressants since they take so long to take effect.

I started bit by bit, day by day, to clean my unit. I could only manage one glass door at the start, then would go back to bed. Eventually, I cleaned the unit and progressed to the swimming pool. I could only manage one lap when I started. However, over the next few months, I was up to seven laps and more just trying to rid myself of the black dog that had decided to hang around my back door.

One month went by, then another and then another. At least my flat was clean. Then, just by chance, I ran into an acquaintance at the shopping centre who asked about my welfare. I explained that I was currently unemployed. He inquired if I would like a job and I said, "Sure, what sort of job is it?" He replied, "Driving trucks; have you got a truck license? It's up at Pormpurraw. Can you handle it?"

It had been many years since I'd driven a truck. However, I didn't think it would take me that long to reacquaint myself with the gears again. I was duly employed within a week and shortly after that, I was on a plane headed for Pormpurraw. I've never been to Pormpurraw in my entire life. To make things just a little more complicated, my dad became very ill just before I was due to fly out. Unsure of what to do, I phoned him and he said, "Go ahead and take the job. Don't worry about me. I'll be alright." They were famous last words. Technically, he died midflight to Brisbane. However, for the grace of God, he came back to this world and is still with us to this day as I write this book.

I've been in some rough camps and have been around some rough people in my life. However, Pormpurraw was like taking one leaf out of the book called *Hell*. The only communication we had was a satellite phone in the main office. If we had a good mobile, we could drive about 20km up the road and get reasonable reception. I started work straight away pumping water out of Toby's Lagoon into a truck with a big water tank and then into two tanks for use in the camp.

The heat was so intense that it drained every ounce of energy I had. My lower back started to cause me grief on the first day. I mentioned earlier in the book that I was born with spondylolisthesis and the seat in the truck just didn't agree with my condition. By Day Two, I was in hell. The pain was so intense that I had to put one leg under my backside to try propping myself up. Day in and day out, I had the worst pain I've ever experienced in my life.

Fortunately, there was someone in the camp with similar back problems. He had an electric massager like the ones they use professionally. I would borrow it every night, whenever he wasn't using it. But the pain went on and was relentless. I was taking Neurofin in very dangerous doses yet I still wasn't getting relief. I got to the point where I thought about taking my life. I started to think about it throughout the day. I wondered about how I could do it and make it look like an accident. However, I knew from the work I had already studied from the Researchers of Truth that there would be no peace for me on the other side, if I chose that path.

I finally found a way that would help me leave this world looking like I'd had an accident. I pumped water to be used on the road out of a lagoon on a creek, about 15 km from where we were working. The water tank of the truck had a partition with a hole through it to help stop the surge of water upon acceleration and braking. The hole was just big enough for a person to fit through. I figured if I started the water pump and pumped water to the water tank of the truck, I'd be able to slide through the hole in the partition. The water would slowly fill, I'd be trapped and would die by drowning.

The moment I found what I thought was the perfect way out, I didn't want to die anymore. Even though the rest of the world would see it like an accident, I knew deep within me that I would always know what I had done and taken the easy way out. Christ would always know what I had done. Suicide is never the way.

The pain didn't go away. Every time we had a break and flew into Cairns, I sought the help of every medical discipline I could think of. I started with a chiropractor, a Japanese deep massage therapist; and an acupuncturist. I also sought help from a psychologist to see if my mind could be reprogrammed to handle the pain and eventually stumbled upon a helpful physiotherapist.

The physiotherapist I sought out, also suffered from spondylolisthesis. He was able to give me specific exercises to strengthen my lower back muscles. Within two weeks, the pain was starting to lift and within six weeks, I was getting close to normal.

I managed to get a phone call in. I found out that my dad had survived his trip to Brisbane and was recovering from his ordeal. One of the truck drivers in the camp quit his position. I was offered his job driving a Mack semi-trailer hauling 38 tons of road dressing. I hadn't driven a semi-trailer for nearly 40 years. I was instructed to drive this one without disengaging the clutch and to change gears just by picking the revs. It took me weeks to get close to even being a half-reasonable driver.

This is where the heat really started to take its toll. The air conditioning wasn't working in the truck and when working with the road dressing, the dust was so intense I had to have both truck windows rolled up. One afternoon around 2 PM, we got a thermometer and measured the heat inside the truck. The mercury read 48°C. We were forever running out of cool water by mid-afternoon and what was cool in the morning was now hot. Drinking hot water doesn't have much effect on quenching the thirst.

It was a rough camp, and that's an understatement. There were about 15 men, all working in the heat of road building that went from Pormpuraaw right into the heart of Cape York Peninsula, Queensland Australia. This road was an offshoot of the main arterial road for the Cape named the Peninsula Development Road or as the locals would say, the PRD.

The one thing that sticks in my mind more than any other of my stays in that camp, were the trips that I made to Toby's Lagoon in the water truck. For some strange reason, this huge lagoon had a peacefulness and serenity to it that I haven't found in many places in Australia. The weirdest part is that a young boy, around four years of age, drowned in that lagoon some years ago. His parents were from Melbourne and they were on a travelling holiday when the tragedy occurred. For whatever reason, this place feels tranquil to be in. There is no spookiness and nothing like that at all. There is just tranquility.

The funniest part was my very first day on the job when they put me on the water truck and sent me off to Toby's Lagoon to get a load of water for the camp. What they didn't tell me, was that the parking brakes on the truck were very second-rate. No, you should make that third rate. When I got out of the truck to hook up the hoses, the truck started careening backwards towards the lagoon. I ran flat out towards the truck, managed to jump in while it was moving and put my foot on the brakes.

What they had forgot to tell me was that I needed to put a big hunk of wood behind the back tyres to stop the truck from rolling back and ending up in the lagoon, since the parking brake was non-existent. Just leaving the truck in gear wasn't enough to hold it, unless it was on level ground. After that incident, my association with Toby's Lagoon was all-peaceful. We even had the odd party there on a Saturday night when we weren't working on a Sunday.

The number one grader driver was a grouchy old bugger who drank heavily every night. How much he drank was measured by how cranky his demeanour was the following day. He won a significant amount of money in the gold lotto and retired for a brief amount of time. However, he longed for the job he had done most of his life, so he went back to it. He bought himself a new truck, drank quite considerably, and then felt the need to go back to his old job. What was so crazy was that he still wasn't happy with his decision. Up until the time I left, he still hadn't reconciled this matter. However, he did take his agression out on all and sundry around him.

There were two grader drivers. The other guy was the complete opposite of the heavy drinker. When he wasn't working on graders in the Cape, he had a little farm that was his pride and joy near Malanda in North Queensland. He had a very kind disposition and I wondered how he fit in with this rough-and-tumble bunch.

He loaned me a book entitled, *Grey Eagle*. The reading of this book was one of the highlights of my stay in this camp. It was about a guy in America who related to American Indians and lived a very similar lifestyle to the Indians trapping beavers. He eventually told himself that he was an American Indian and people came to believe it. To make his red-Indian fantasy even more real, he married a red-Indian woman. When he travelled to England, he was greeted as a Wild West hero. He eventually changed his ways and became a conservationist. He pleaded for help to ensure the survival of beavers in North America. He continued in this vein until his dying day.

What I learned about myself from reading his story is that, although I strongly identify with the Aboriginal culture, I am not and never will be an Aboriginal in this lifetime. This book spelled it out to me in no-uncertain terms. I know I have been an Aboriginal in previous lifetimes and I've seen that quite clearly many times in out-of-body experiences. However, that doesn't make me an Aboriginal in this lifetime. It has enhanced my journey 100 fold and at times confused me earlier in my life, before I was able to have the clarity and understanding that I have today.

Our camp was situated in the middle of nowhere. It had its own power supply, which was a big diesel generator. We carted water from Toby's Lagoon to drink and bathe in. We were about 30 km from Pormpuraaw and about 10 km from Toby's Lagoon. We were just outside the boundary of an enforced alcohol-free area in the township of Pormpurraw. It meant that we could have a beer or two at night after work. Some of the workers interpreted that as 22 beers. As soon as we knocked off work and got our work boots off, it was into the fridge and then it was conversation time. Eventually, different people gathered at different peoples' places (Donga's) to share stories and their beers. I was probably the odd one out, because I didn't drink that much. I set myself a daily limit so I wouldn't fall into the trap that many had fallen into.

I became friends with one guy who was from Torres Strait Island and the quiet grader driver from Malanda. I also made casual friendships with the indigenous guys in the crew. It was one of the most unorthodox gatherings of people I've ever seen in my life. One guy had a girlfriend in town and spent a little time in the camp. There was another guy from TI and he spent a fair amount of time bootlegging grog from the camp into the township. There was another guy who had a sizeable beer belly and was a fellow semi-trailer driver. He used to smoke marijuana in the afternoons just to make the day go quicker. One of the other guys on the excavator, was up to the very same trick and he was loading our trucks.

One semi-trailer driver was a private contractor. He always came across as thinking he was one better than the rest of us. Some years later, while working for a medical service in Cairns, I spotted him in the psychiatric ward of the Cairns Base Hospital. He seemed to be of the opinion that I should be in his place. I had a good laugh and left him in a better place.

There was also the camp cook. I'm sure I could write a book on him alone. He was the strangest mix of a person I've met in all my years on planet Earth. Slim Dusty recorded a song called, "The Drovers Cook" and the comparisons between the man and that song and our cook were quite significant. He was someone who spent most of his waking hours in a fantasyland. His stories varied on the day he told them and to whom he was telling them.

Although he wasn't second in charge, in many instances he took this role upon himself. The actual boss was hundreds of kilometres away in a place called Townsville. About once a month, he paid a visit but never really connected with the men. Most of the gear was secondhand and breakdowns happened regularly.

The food was passable. The only problem was that the menu stayed very much the same. If we had pork chops Thursday this week we would, more than likely, have pork chops the following Thursday. This pattern was repeated over the months. We had to organise our own lunches, which we did in the early morning before or after breakfast. There was not a lot to choose from, so we had to make do with whatever was on offer. It was either that or go on a weight-reduction program.

We would wake around 4:30 AM, have a shower, shave, get dressed, put the steel-cap work boots on, then partake of breakfast. After lunches were done, if we were lucky, we'd fill our water bottle for the day with water and ice. The ice was available on a 50-50 basis: one day it was there, the next it wasn't. Working in an intensely hot environment, we really needed to hydrate regularly. We were driving our trucks out of the camp just as the first rays of daylight appeared. We drove by lights to the worksite and by the time we got there, daybreak was occurring. We generally started work before 6 AM and most days worked a

10-hour day, 7 days a week, though every second Sunday we got to finish at lunchtime.

We had a roster of 14 days on and 4 days off. In those times, we were given free air transport back to Cairns. Those four days used to fly by as if they were two and sometimes the plane didn't even come to pick us up. This was because the charter company chose a different charter that was paying more money than ours. You can just imagine what is was like for this entire crew to be at the airport waiting, waiting and waiting with no plane coming to get them. A few abusive calls were exchanged on mobile phones. We'd then go back to the camp to bide our time until the next fly out.

After seven months, I had enough of the crazy cook, the dust, the isolation, and the men who regularly had sexual talks regarding other men, the heat, the flies, and my chronic bad back. I handed in my notice and in 24 hours, I was out of there. My lower back pain hasn't magically disappeared but I have taken much more control over my own destiny by engaging in Pilates and working out at the local gym to strengthen my lower back muscles.

While I suffered the most extreme pain I'd ever known in my life, I also learned the biggest lesson I would ever learn in my life. There never is an excuse or a reason to take one's own life. This lesson would catapult me into the most spiritually productive period of my life.

Many travel the path seeking a teacher, a guru, the wisdom of the wise old woman, and many don't seek till they're nearly knocking on death's door. I was one of those that sought a teacher, a guru or anyone that could lead me to the Light. After a lifetime of searching, I found the teacher I was looking for: The Teacher who awakens us from within our inner selves.

Another teacher came my way by an old, old story that gets better every time I retell it. A long, long time ago there lived in the forest a wise old woman. Many had heard about her but few had the privilege to share her company. One day, a young woman called Rosie dared to go deep into the dark forest. It was further than those before had ventured. She could see a shadowy figure in the distance and her heart started to race. One part of her was telling her to turn and retreat quickly and yet the other part was telling her to press on.

As she got closer to the shadowy figure, it became clear to her that this woman was very, very old. By her calculations, the old woman could easily be 200 years of age. Her silvery hair shone in what little light came through the canopy of the rainforest and was so long that it nearly touched the ground.

Rosie greeted the old woman, who responded similarly. She noticed a pile of shimmering jewels next to the where the old woman sat. The old woman observed where Rosie's attention was and offered her any jewel she desired out of the pile. She was instantly drawn to a diamond nearly as big as her closed fist and then happily departed down the same road she came. This diamond, when traded, would allow her to live a life of luxury for the rest of her days.

Some weeks went by and Rosie made the trek back to see the old woman. The old woman questioned the purpose of her trip and asked if the diamond had been unsuitable. She assured her the diamond was more than she could ever ask for. The old woman then asked why she came back and Rosie said, "I want some of what you have that enabled you to give away the diamond in the first place."

I had a tidy sum of money saved up from my long service leave from Radio BBM and my work at Pormpurraw, so I had a couple of weeks' break before I started looking for another job. It didn't take long and when my stars aligned, I went for a job as a Mental Health worker at Wuchopperen Medical Service. I also applied for a job driving a tractor slashing grass on the side of the road and another job driving a truck for Alsco Linen.

I went for the interview at Wuchopperen and before I reached my home, I had a phone call offering me the job that I took without hesitation. I had absolutely no prior work experience or training in mental health but for whatever the reason, I was offered the job. This was an indigenous organisation as well and for the second time in my life, my white-skin colour was not a barrier.

The other two organisations offered me a job on the very same day but I stayed with my original job acceptance at Wuchopperen. From memory, the job interview was on a Wednesday and I started in my new role the following Monday on 16 December 2008.

My work involved working with people who had mental health issues. The role was rather broad and much of it was left up to us to work it out there and then. One of my first tasks was to drive a lady with some mental health concerns. She also had a damaged hip and needed a walking stick. This was quite a task for her. I was about to find out how big a task on our first outing. I picked her up, drove into the shopping centre, and pulled up in the nearest available car space where she got out and started to walk as best she could towards the shopping centre. As this was such a huge task for her, that she quickly became very angry, yelled at me to get f'd, and proceeded to make her way home by herself with agony. The next time I took her out, I pulled the vehicle right up in front of the shopping centre entrance which she was very pleased with.

Each client had different problems that we had to deal with. One particular lady liked to smoke a lot of marijuana and was very prone to aggression when things weren't going her way. Many of the clients loved to get out of town and see a bit of country so we would often take them for a drive. Sometimes, the greater part of the drive would be in silence and I respected that.

Not long after starting my employment, I was fishing around looking for a particular book in my bookcase when I picked up *Fire in the Heart* by Kyriacos Markides. This book was the third of a trilogy that Kyriacos had written about a healer from Cyprus called Daskalos. I had read the previous two several years before and upon reading *Fire in the Heart* for the second time, a spiritual fire exploded within me.

The effect that Daskalos has had on my life and continues to have, is beyond any words I can put on these pages. It is beyond life changing. I was soon seeking some connection to the source, which I found in the legacy he left behind called The Researchers of Truth.

I found the website and discovered that his daughter, Panayiota, had dedicated much of her life to making the teachings of her father available to everyone via CDs, books, and later by direct MP3 download from the *Researchers of Truth Website*. I died and went to heaven! I had been seeking someone like Daskalos all my life and strangely, at the same time, I started having more and more contact with indigenous traditional healers in Cairns. I began working with them and working with clients suffering from mental health issues.

I purchased nearly every available CD from Panayiota, bought every book that was available, and then started a five-year journey that has now turned into a 10-year effort studying *The Symbol of Life*. This is deeply profound esoteric work and I'm going over it for the second time, just in case I missed something the first time.

I have always meditated at various times throughout my life but now with Panayiota's guidance, it became a daily affair. I finally came to put a name to what I had been experiencing over time: out-of-body-experiences (OBE). I had been having these experiences throughout my life. Now with the help of Daskalos and Panayiota, I learned how to bring about an OBE consciously and how to control it. I am able to be thousands of kilometres away and yet come back into my body in a second.

Every night after dinner, I would now reflect on what I had said and done during the day (called introspection). I learned about the five keys to the kingdoms of the heavens. Many of the things I learned were simply re-learning from previous lifetimes. I already knew about materialisation and dematerialisation but I didn't know what it was called. I was afraid to tell anyone. I was about to commence a journey that has no end. In fact, the journey had begun many lifetimes ago.

Mark Matouse had this to say a few months before Daskalos died, "The 83-year-old Spyros Sathi, widely regarded as the greatest Christian mystic of modern times, agreed to sit down and talk with me in his first American interview. Known simply as the Daskalos ('teacher'), this powerful Cypriot healer had, I'd heard, once frightened a group of hard-nosed reporters by rocking a lame child in his arms and setting him down a few minutes later on legs that were suddenly functional. The night before our interview, I'd studied the Daskalos from a distance, holding forth on a New York stage strewn with flowers; now, stepping into his hotel room with a photographer, I had no idea what to expect."

"The moment he rose—six feet five in a cardigan sweater—and took my hand, all my apprehension disappeared. Something about this towering man—a glowing kindness, a welcoming ease—put me at ease, too, and for the next hour, I questioned him about how it felt to have his powers. I barely understood his responses (you try interviewing a mystic), but when I stood up to say goodbye, I was so light-headed—so light all over—that I had to sit down to steady myself. The Daskalos smiled and watched me intently; then without any forethought, I asked him about a painful situation in my life. My host leaned forward, took my wrist between his fingers, and said, 'You are good'. Three simple words—just that—bearing no conscious link to my question; yet hearing them I wanted to weep, as if Spyros Sathi had somehow heard, underneath the surface question, a deeper confusion, a covert hunger, a secret longing to be blessed. The photographer happened to capture this moment, the Daskalos gently touching my arm, grinning at me as I beamed back at him with the same sort of lit-up expression. In the photograph, which I treasure, my face looks like a hundred-watt bulb".

"I've never been a person of faith. In matters of spirit, I'm from Missouri—fascinated but skeptical. Were it not for meeting the Daskalos and a handful of other exceptional teachers in my travels as a writer and seeker, I would surely doubt that such a thing as spiritual energy existed—not as a miraculous fluke but a natural gift accessible to all of us. Like harmony, symmetry, and even genius, this invisible force is a mystery whose uplifting power must be encountered to be believed. Once that happens, revealing a glimpse of our awesome potential, it can never again be denied".

CHAPTER 8

THE ROAD HOME

I'm 61 years of age. Since the day I was born, I have been preparing for my journey home. Everything I've ever done and everything I've ever said has been in preparation for this event. Every twist and turn, every fork in the road, every bad roll of the dice, every vision, every meditation, every out-of-body experience, every dream and every waking moment, they've all been preparing me for the road home.

I've been aware of a world I'm going to since a very young age. For me, the dream world was just an extension of everyday life. I didn't understand every dream but many times, I could remember it in every tiny detail. I later became aware that many of my dreams were just remembering my past incarnations. It was the same for my out-of-body experiences. I thought everybody did it. I've been flying, having out-of-body experiences for over 50 years now and the details keep getting clearer.

I recently flew (OBE) to the Sphinx in Egypt, more exactly to the right paw of the Sphinx. At the same time, I could see the dust coming up off the desert sands. It took me back to an incarnation that I had as a Bedouin. I can remember the type of tents we erected at night, the oasis we would visit, the sweet dates we ate and right down to the smell of the camels.

The Researchers of Truth teach through meditation led by Panayiota Atteshlis, how you can contact your archangels, how to still the mind, right down to meditations on the nine divine rays. While meditating on the sixth Divine Ray, I finally got to see the six squares of pure white light that I saw in a vision on the wall of the house in Deniliquin in 1983 that started a journey I haven't yet completed. Those six squares spoke to me and I listened, resigned my position at the radio station, and packed up the family and travelled back to North Queensland. 30 years later in 1993, I finally got to see those six squares of pure white light once more.

Between purchasing CDs and books and downloading material from Panayiota's website, I purchased a small bookcase full of her material and Daskalos'. I have been truly blessed to receive what she and her father have so richly shared with the rest of the world. Some days I feel like I have been given two days for the price of one.

While meditating on the eighth Divine Ray, I travelled to the world beyond this one. There I was given a gift of diamonds and gold that filled the back of a semitrailer. The diamonds were bigger than oranges. I picked up one, opened it, and drank what was within: Living Water, a gift straight from God. It illustrates that in the world beyond this one, diamonds and gold are worthless although we value them here on the earth plane.

One of the reasons I don't often go to the movies is because my dream world is so rich. I have dreams far beyond what is shown on the movie screens. Someone once said to me, "Let your dreams run wild and may you be brave enough to follow."

In the world beyond, you can be exactly how you want to be. For instance, if you pass over at 81 years of age and would like people on the other side to recognise how you looked at 40, then that is exactly how you will look. You can be as young or as old as you choose to be. In the end, you will probably more than likely come to the conclusion that it doesn't matter one way or another in the other world.

In the astral world/the world beyond/The Dreamtime, everything is very luminous. Light emanates from absolutely everything. There is no need for a sun or a moon. The horses run on top of the clouds or you can have them do whatever you want. If you prefer a car, it will fly through the air, too, if that is what you want. You'll never need to fill it up with gas again. I saw a car like this suspended in mid-air on the front album of a band called the Ozark Mountain Daredevils over 40 years ago. This album cover has kept me enthralled until I was able to enter that world. Perhaps, the band had a glimpse of what it is like in the worlds beyond. The album was called *The Car Over the Lake*. Somehow, I always knew that the picture was real, but its reality was in another world.

In some ways, the astral world is also here on this planet. The Aboriginal people of Australia have the best terminology to describe these worlds. They simply call it the Dreamtime. Their interpretation means that it's possible to access this dream world not only in waking hours, fully conscious, but while asleep as well. In the Dreamtime, it's possible to see and talk with deceased relatives. It is possible not only to see them but also to have a meaningful conversation with them and to be guided by them.

This other world can also manifest itself on this dimension as a vision. Just recently, I had the good fortune to visit an Aboriginal tourist destination near Mossman in North Queensland. I was thoroughly engrossed in the stories being told, when I noticed up ahead a group of Aboriginal people around a fireplace under an overhanging rock. I asked the guide if those people were there to entertain the tourists and the guide replied, "There's no one there but there used to be thousands of years ago as that rock overhang provided shelter and they were able to have a fire." I was fully lucid and yet able to go back thousands of years in time and see life as it was then. The guide was unperturbed by my revelation since that's the kind of thing Aboriginal people are familiar with. However, much of that is being eroded away with the intrusion of modern civilisation.

Some of this erosion has eked its way into the once holy domain of the Traditional Aboriginal healer. These healers were once an integral part of everyday Aboriginal life. In some cases, they were feared. This fear chased someone down who had broken the law and if the Kadaitcha Man would point the "bone" at the offender, the person would be dead within a week. However, they did amazing healing work quite similar to the work of Stylianos Atteshlis (Daskalos).

I worked alongside traditional healers during my seven years of employment at an Aboriginal health service. We would pick clients up, take them out bush, and we would smoke them. All the while, the healer would talk in his own tongue and demand that any bad spirits be on their way.

I even worked with the healers in the psychiatric care unit of the Cairns Base Hospital. I sought the permission of three senior psychiatrists to be able to do this. The document they signed is proudly displayed on a wall in my home. This line of thought runs against much of what a modern psychiatrist is trained to do. However, because they had exhausted all other options, they felt a duty to their patients to try other avenues.

In one visit, a trainee psychiatrist wanted to see what the traditional healers were doing. In fact, he was very skeptical and asked if it was okay to see the healer at work. The healer went about his job and pulled from the neck of a patient, a stingray barb (bone). The trainee psychiatrist saw him pull the barb out of the neck. He got such a shock that his facial expression was as if he had seen a ghost. He was so taken aback that he left the scene in a hurry. I was privy to work with nearly every Traditional Healer that lived in Cairns in that seven-year period along with some that lived out of town.

Each and every one took me under their wing. They explained what they were doing and how they were doing it, the plants they used, the words infused with power that were used to chase away bad spirits and everything I could possibly comprehend. I was their apprentice and a willing one at that. I never lost sight of the greatest healer there ever was: Christ and, with Him, I communicate every day.

When I started this book, I was seeking self-realisation. Now on my way home, I yearn for Theosis, if it be His will (At-one-ment with the God, the Absolute Beingness). According to Nisargadatta Mahara, "The search for reality is the most dangerous of all undertakings, for it destroys the world in which you live."

Apart from the first two Commandments (of Love), the most important words in my life come from the Scriptures and those words are, "All these things you shall do and more."

"All things are possible; the magic has always been within you," is one of my favourite quotes. It then becomes possible for a psychotherapist to cure people, become a mental healer, and cure with authority and cooperation with the Holy Spirit. All things are possible.

An Archangel once told me I was moving through a time of transformation. The Archangel said I have been preparing for this moment and other angels were waiting to help guide me on my path. I was afraid to heal others, because I was afraid to fail. Then a few years ago, the brother of someone I went to high school with 47 years ago spoke to my dad after church and mentioned how his brother had had a very severe surfing accident.

I knew my time had come. I asked Dad to contact this fellow the next opportunity he had at church and ask him for his brother's phone number. Dad did this and passed the number on to me. I phoned David and inquired if I could be of assistance. I offered to perform distance healing on him, if he agreed. He replied he didn't believe in God or any of that "stuff". I assured him that all he had to do was to agree for me to work on him.

He wore a steel neck brace. He had a broken neck and was in incredible pain. This was my first serious healing work and I regularly sent him "balls of light" as instructed in the meditation for distance healing by Panayiota Atteshlis of the Researchers of Truth. I contacted David a number of times and assured him I was continuing to send him light. He told me that he had recently sold a property to a coalmine company in Central Queensland. He had come into some millions of dollars and offered me $200,000. He said, "You can have as much as you want."

News of his healing was relayed to me when he bumped into another friend of mine in Emerald and told him of the healing work that I was doing. He also told my friend that he thought I must be quite mad because I didn't take the large sum of money he offered me. The second friend passed the message onto my dad and I'm quite sure the second friend had similar thoughts as David had in regards to my sanity and the way I knocked back his money.

I knew this was my first big test. I also knew that if I refused the money, my healing powers would increase, which they have. I have done other distance healings since then. For every healing I perform, Jesus Christ appears to me while I'm in meditation. He doesn't look like the picture-perfect images as shown on the wall scenes of most churches. The Christ I see is quite ruddy in complexion with a darker skin than those usually portrayed of him. Once I see him, I know the healing is complete.

There are a growing number of people who have had a direct experience of Jesus. They declare that there is no "Second Coming" because Christ the Saviour is already here. Many people feel they were unworthy to be healed. Others feel that they need to pay a lot of money. Before healing the many he healed, Jesus quite often said, "Your sins have been forgiven." We don't need to be forgiven again to receive healing as he forgave all our sins on the cross.

This is the end of my journey to date and the most significant thing that I have learned is that I'm now able to offer healing to anyone in need.

There is no fee, just come in faith.

You can contact me in Australia via email on
shaman7775555@gmail.com

And, if possible, include a picture of yourself or whoever it is that needs help.

Thank you for sharing my journey.

Accept what is,
Let go of what was,
And have faith in what will be.
(Buddah)

Dharayara (aka Gregory Wallace Reid)
2016 Australia

QR code of my Website